Religion and . . .

By Leo Sandon

To Bob Evans, for over 48 years of friendship. Thank you for looking after Marvel Lou and me.

Leo Sandon
4 July 2014

Selections from "Religion in America," 1985–2001

first published by the *Tallahassee Democrat*

Manufactured in the United States of America
10 09 08 07 06 05 04 03 02 01
5 4 3 2 1

Designer and Typesetter: Karen Towson Wells
Typefaces: Bell and Zebrawood Regular
Printer and binder: Durraprint

Library of Congress Cataloging-in-Publivcation Date
Leo Sandon

ISBN 1-889574-13-9

Sentry Press
424 East Call Street
Tallahassee, Florida 32301-7693

To the Memory of my Parents
Grace Rebecca and Leo

Foreword

Writing this foreword gives me enormous pleasure for I have long been an admirer of those scholars like Leo Sandon who assume the challenges and burdens of the role of public intellectual in American society outside the confines of sometimes arcane academic discourse. It is particularly crucial for scholars of religion to assume this role because their discipline has much to contribute to a proper understanding of a society suffused with diverse religious traditions affecting virtually all aspects of social and cultural life. Indeed, literacy in America's religions seems prerequisite to maintaining our mutual respect for one another's religious liberty and freedom of conscience, since this civic value can be so easily undermined by ignorance and resultant religious prejudice and intolerance.

The scholar of religion, then, can serve an important role in our society and culture as mediator between the academic study of religion and citizens who may need expert guidance in understanding religious worldviews and practices with which they are unfamiliar. Moreover, such a mediator is especially well-positioned to alert all of us to the nuances of significant public issues affected by deeply held religious and moral beliefs: in this respect, the public intellectual can enhance public debate about matters pertaining to our common weal. In my view, Leo Sandon, in his column, rises to the challenge of this crucial mediating role by putting his extensive knowledge of religions in America in the service of the public community. Taken together, his selected individual columns accomplish this task in three ways. First, they offer, within the constraints of a newspaper column to be sure, a short course in religion in America, ranging across diverse traditions (e.g., Christianity, Islam,

Judaism) and variants from within them (e.g., Roman Catholicism, African American Churches, religious fundamentalism, types of Judaism). Second, the sheer scope of his topics demonstrate just how deeply religious ideas, impulses, and practices shape virtually all aspects of our lives together (e.g., sports, politics, film, gender relations, legal rulings, national calamities). Third, the columns do not shy away from offering critical insight on important and controversial issues of the day (e.g., AIDS policy, death penalty, abortion, religious infringement, church-state relations, religious politics).

One can only be grateful to Leo Sandon for his willingness to share with us how his academic background and research critically illuminate so much that we experience and think about in our daily and public lives together as citizens of a complex, rich, pluralistic, and sometimes puzzling republic.

Sumner B. Twiss, Distinguished Professor of
Human Rights, Ethics, and Religion
The Florida State University

Table of Contents

Sport

Holidays

National Calamities

Policy Issues

The State

Film

Judaisms in America

Roman Catholicism in America

The Black Church in America

Gender

Politics

Islam in America

Pluralist America

The Fundamentalist Mentality

Index

Preface

When it was suggested to me that I choose a number of my *Religion in America* columns for publication as an anthology I had doubts concerning the wisdom of such a project. Journalistic pieces tend to have brief shelf life. This seemed especially true for a column which had been running for over sixteen years. It is one thing to read a column over Saturday morning coffee, another to read one published on a Saturday morning ten years ago. I trust that those who first invited me to publish *Religion and...* knew what they were about. I should acknowledge that the urging of other friends and colleagues also provided encouragement to assemble this anthology.

One of the most gratifying experiences of my professional life has been the positive response to the column from readers who do not as a habit follow religious news." A frequent preface to comments I receive regarding the column is "I usually do not read the religion page, but I read your column when it appears." This prelude is itself a compliment (whatever the person may proceed to say) because I write to suggest to the "I am not religious, but ..." group that religion is connected to more aspects of our lives than we think. And these connections, once identified and described, are often quite interesting. I write also for more conventionally religious persons, hoping to offer new ways of looking at familiar aspects of their world. The distribution of the column on the Knight Ridder Tribune wire service has provided for wider national and even international exposure which also has been exicting. It is gratifying, finally, to receive negative responses to the columns because I know that I am, at the least, making contact, at the best often standing corrected and seeing points I hadn't seen before. The column, then, is increasingly expanding in scope and increasingly interactive in character.

The title and organization of the book perhaps comes close to belaboring the obvious point that my primary interest as teacher and writer is the interaction between religion and culture. I received the traditional doctoral training emphasizing the dissertation and the monograph characterized by original research and controlling expertise in a relatively narrow area. My major focus was intellectual history, focusing on twentieth-century religious thought—theology—in the United States. Over the years I expanded this original concentration to research, writing and teaching in social history. This broadening continued with interdisciplinary and cross-disciplinary courses I taught in connection with my quarter-century directorship of Florida State University's Program in American Studies. In these latter days, then, my principal interest and activity increasingly has been in cultural studies. This emphasis is reflected in the "Religion in America" column, the major journalistic component of my writing. *Religion and...*, therefore, is an appropriate way of conceptualizing and organizing this anthology.

One major and enduring theme in my columns is that of religious pluralism. A pastor in the Tallahassee area purportedly said from the pulpit, "Leo Sandon isn't loyal to the Lord Jesus Christ, he is loyal to pluralism." The preacher was, at least partially, insightful. I do indeed believe that the primary religious reality in the United States is diversity and that is not a viewpoint I only recently reached. I also believe that religious traditions have their own pluralist character, acknowledged or unacknowledged. These pluralist components, therefore, are found within religious groups as well as among them. I have tried to nudge readers to realize that our nation and its specific faith communities are pluralistic and to urge them to affirm that fact with policies—the ideology, if you will—of plural*ism*.

A corollary theme in my columns, however, is that it is possible to be both a committed member of a faith community and genuinely open to other such communities. Responding to the preacher's alleged identification of my "disloyalty" in Christological terms in the quotation above, I can only say that many years ago I reached the conclusion that it is possible to believe that God is revealed conclusively in Jesus Christ without having to believe that God is revealed exclusively in Jesus Christ. When I think as a Christian I do not join those of my tradition who reduce all theology to Christology. As a professor of religion in a state university, furthermore, with department colleagues whose training and academic expertise entail all world religions, I have had the opportunity to visit—to "pass over" to—other traditions, and I have been enriched by the travel. This confessional theme, finally, follows naturally from my conviction that no human being can be in possession of absolute truth. Reality may indeed be one, but finite creatures experience it as plurality. Some of us might believe in the Absolute— "The Lord our God, the Lord is one"—but our knowledge of the Absolute One is not itself absolute.

I am aware that the term "America" when writing primarily about the United States is problematic. Many insist that "the Americas" should be substituted as the inclusive term for all nations in the Western Hemisphere. I have changed the title of my undergraduate liberal studies course, for instance, from "Religion in America" to "Religion in the United States." Some academicians might argue that I likewise should have changed the title of my newspaper column. While in one sense such a change would be an appropriate nod to political correctness (a category which, for me, is neither pejorative nor a reference of ridicule), there is another sense in which "America" and "American" are peculiar as symbolic metaphors for the meaning of the United States's experience. I retain "America," not only in deference to popular, commonplace usage, but out of a conviction that it has legitimacy as a special concept—and idea—as well as an objective, descriptive one. "America," in this second sense, means the system(s) of cultural ideas and symbols which provide terms of identity and cohesion for interpreting the United States, past and present.

Before reviewing over sixteen years of columns, I had not realized how many words *Religion in America* has used. The choice of columns is arbitrary, though not random. The anthology constitutes a relatively small sampling of almost 400 columns. I resisted temptations to re-write or to update the columns. Journalists live easily with one-sentence paragraphs: academicians usually experience them with more discomfort. There has been an occasional conflation of paragraphs. With the exception of correcting minor copy-editing errors and several factual mistakes, they appear as they were published.

Leo Sandon
Tallahassee, Florida
December 7, 2001

Acknowledgments

I am indebted to Florida State University's Emeritus Professor of History William W. Rogers for initially suggesting that these columns be published by Sentry Press. Professor Rogers, director of Sentry, has guided the publication of the anthology with sure hand and steady encouragement. Karen Wells, production manager of Sentry Press, has been efficient, capable, and a joy to work with.

I am indebted to the *Tallahassee Democrat* for publishing "Religion in America" since 1985, and particularly to Judy Doyle, the current religion page editor. The person who has edited most of the columns from the beginning has been the *Democrat's* Ron Hartung. Without Ron the column would neither have gotten launched nor contined through the years. We have worked together through several stages of technology, the earliest of which was rather primitive and hand-delivery oriented. We have developed a relationship that is smooth to the point of being alter ego in character. Ron is editor par excellence.

The person who has kept the project on schedule is Lawrence Webster, librarian, information services consultant, and my graduate research assistant for the academic year, 2001-2002. Grace abounding! She really has functioned as something of a consulting editor for this volume. I will always be grateful that our paths crossed when they did.

I acknowledge the encouragement and support of President Talbot "Sandy" D'Alemberte and Dean Donald J. Foss of Florida State's College of Arts and Sciences. Sandy and his wife Patsy are friends of long standing who believe "writing out" to the general public is a useful enterprise for a university professor. Dean Foss's support has been invaluable. Their affirmation of my work is much appreciated.

I have been blessed, finally, to be in our Department of Religion which tolerates journalistic activity as well as more conventional scholarly enterprise.

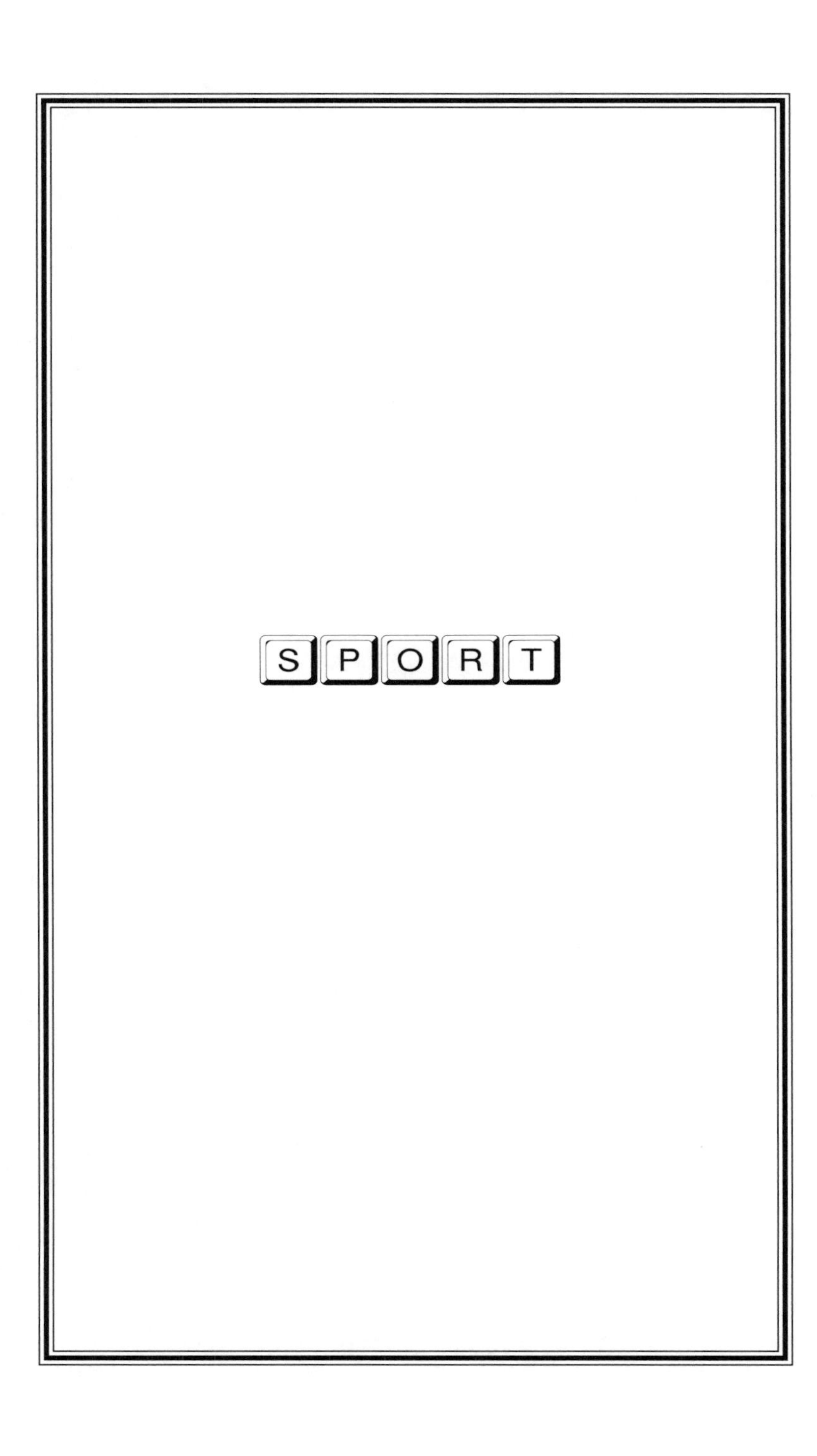
SPORT

Sport

"It's that time: the great American football ritual" was the first *Religion in America* column. Although it was ostensibly football specific, it was as much about the role of sport in society in general. Football has long been important in Tallahassee, but even at that, this piece, written in August, 1985, was published at what turned out to be the beginning of an incredible period for Florida State University football. For fourteen years FSU was numbered among the top five teams in the nation. In the decade of the 1990s Coach Bobby Bowden's teams had the most consistently successful record in major college football, including two national championships.

My interest in sport was initially academic in nature. As a religion professor and an Americanist I became interested in the role of sport in American culture and religion and developed an American Studies lecture series course, "Sport in America." In 1984 I chaired a special university committee that produced what, up until then, was the most thorough study that any Division I-A school had made with regard to its student athletes. These activities, coupled with the fact that the first column was scheduled for August 31, 1985, made the topic timely. Various aspects of sport and religion was a subject to which I returned a number of times.

My two-fold typology for dealing with the subject has been "religion *in* sport" and "sport *as* religion." The first classification refers to the incidence of sectarian religious activity in sport, the second to the manner in which sport functions in ways similar to religion, indeed even sometimes as a surrogate religion.

The piece on the coming of football season in Tallahassee is a case study of sport as religion or at least as "religious." The points are not particularly original. The column lays out generalizations about sport in culture, specifically American culture, which might enable some readers to view major team sports in a new way.

The second selection, "A few lessons from baseball, religion, and life," was a meditation informed by my protracted affair with baseball. Baseball, with its serious literary tradition and hoary hold on the nation's memory, is the sport of choice for many Americanists. I have been surprised with baseball's enduring place in our sense of national identity and of its apparent resurgence in popularity of late. Particularly since September 11, 2001. This column commends baseball as an aid to religious reflection.

The third column, "Spirit and sport: the vital link," deals not so much with religion in sport or sport as religion, but rather with the point at which these two expressions of the human spirit intersect. It appeared on the day of the Florida State-Florida football game at the conclusion of a season in which Florida State went undefeated and then won the 1999 national championship in the Sugar Bowl. Against the backdrop of the "big game" I referred to a very unrepresentative American sport: trail hiking (Americans are more oriented toward spectator team sports than individual sports such as trail hiking or cross-country skiing). I hope the linkage of the two types of sport supplied by the notions of commitment and mindfulness works. It does for me.

It's that time: the great American football ritual

Some critics have referred to football stadiums as "oval temples," and to our Saturday night fever as "pigskin piety." Bumper stickers proclaim, "Have you thanked our coach today?" and "Hail, St. Bowden!" Football is no religion, of course, but it may serve as a surrogate religion for many secularists. No thoughtful analyst argues that sport deals with the ultimate questions of human life addressed by the major world religions. Still, it functions in a number of ways usually associated with religion. This is particularly true of football in the 1980s.

Both religion and sport include heroes and heroines, shrines, pilgrimages, fanatical believers, testimony, rituals, myths and mysticism. Both celebrate and legitimate a society's most important values. In religious rituals, the repetition of certain symbolic acts reminds worshipers of important beliefs they share with others participating in the liturgy. Similarly, our games are rituals that reveal much about our national character: "By their games ye shall know them." Sometime in the late 1950s or early 1960s, football became the national game. Baseball is now the sport we associate with "the good old days," while football represents the here and now.

It celebrates such contemporary American values as sanctioned violence, specialization, corporate effort rather than individual performance, and commercialization. "Violence" is a multifaceted term: violent hurricanes, violent crime, violent warfare. To hurl a pedestrian to the pavement on Tennessee Street is probably criminal assault. A linebacker behaving the same way in Doak Campbell Stadium is involved in socially sanctioned violence. There is little doubt that physical contact is an attractive part of football for most Americans. Religion, too, has been the source of sanctioned violence—from the institution of holy war in ancient Israel, to Catholic principles of just war, to authorized executions for heresy or criminal acts. Another characteristic of contemporary football and modern times is specialization. We no longer know triple-threat players in a game that comprises specialty teams.

The emphasis on corporate effort in football is greater than in baseball. We Americans are not rugged individualists when it comes to our preferences in sport. We are more attracted to team events than are Europeans and Japanese. There's also much evidence that American religious life is more group participation than solitary pilgrimage. Industrial, bureaucratic, military, religious and football teamwork all have a common cultural frame.

In a capitalist society, sport is bound to be as commercialized as all other social activities. The line between amateur and professional is so murky that few can tell the difference. Many of the evils of modern sport, particularly football, can be traced to excessive commercialization. The same generalization is often true of religion.

The traditional religious vision is of the beloved community. Sport, particularly football, now generates its own sense of community in an increasingly fragmented culture.

The American philosopher Josiah Royce maintained that community comes from persons joined in loyalty to a common cause. A stadium functions like a medieval cathedral—or, to use a more American image, the tailgating at the stadium may be the contemporary equivalent of the nineteenth-century camp meeting.

Those who cannot be there can experience it through the tabernacle that sits in some corner of every American home communicating reality—the television set. The single event that most Americans will experience together this year is the Super Bowl game.

Today, the grand liturgy begins again. In the weeks ahead we will tend to the Great American Football Ritual. We will celebrate both who we are—warts and all—and what we think is important. As we shout and scream, it might be wise to remember that the fortunes of the season are of something less than ultimate importance.

—August 31, 1985

A few lessons from baseball, religion and life

OMAHA

"You're actually going on a pilgrimage," responded the student on the front row of my religion class. That was her interpretation of the announcement of my hastily planned trip; I had admitted that I was going to attend the NCAA College World Series. I traded my accumulated SkyMiles for a round-trip ticket to Omaha, deciding to do what I had wanted to do for several years. So here I am at Rosenblatt Stadium exchanging the world of schedules, appointments, and meetings for one that is not bounded by time. Baseball has its own rhythm. To get into it one has to abandon regular time, declaring, "I don't care if I ever get back."

For me baseball provides, among other things, a framework for personal reflection and spiritual exploration. My student got it right. I guess I am on something of a pilgrimage. For those of us in religious and cultural studies it is a commonplace acknowledgment that games, were, in their origins, religious rituals. One of the characteristics of contemporary sport is that it is ostensibly secular. Another acknowledgment, nevertheless, is that games mirror a society's values—its character. Sport is a microcosm of society. Games are never just games.

I don't want to focus generally on the religion *of* sport or religion *in* sport. A classic example of the former is the Nebraska football fan characterizing the Cornhuskers running onto the field as "life's ultimate experience." The most recent example of the latter is Deion Sanders testifying at a Billy Graham meeting. My subject, rather, is baseball as an aid to spiritual reflection.

As we have watched batting practice on a beautiful weekend afternoon, a friend and avid baseball fan has frequently remarked, "Leo how can anyone watch baseball and not believe there is a God?" It's meant as humor, but it's asked frequently enough to give me pause. I don't believe in baseball as an argument for the existence of God. But I do think it can reinforce religious commitments we may have arrived at on other grounds. Baseball can inform our long-range game plan with its vision of the playing field composed of Euclidean lines and circles with no "territory" to defend, no opponent's territory to penetrate. Our task is to circle the bases and to reach home.

It can teach us to look to the overall average, the longer pattern of performance, rather than becoming overly depressed with one loss or even a series of losses. To suck it up and make the next pitch; to step up and take one's cut. Not bad vision and strategy for *the* pilgrimage.

—June 16, 1999

Spirit and sport: the vital link

Another column about religion in sport? Or sport as religion? Not today.

I am, to be sure, regularly asked about the incidence of organized religious activities in sports: a highly visible chaplain on the sidelines at FSU football games; regular devotions in a number of team sports; possible "church-state" violations; and a general curiosity about the uses and possible abuses of religion in sport. That is an essay I plan to write. But later.

Today's column appears in conjunction with the "game of the season" (if not the decade or century), but I really don't want to talk about the game as religious ritual. And I certainly don't want to discuss it in terms of Armageddon in the Swamp" or speculate on coach Steve Spurrier as anti-Christ.

I want, in a Thoreau-at-Walden-like way, to step back and unearth the essential link between spirit and sport. What is it about participation in sports that makes athletes susceptible to religious overtures? How does religion function in sport?

Sport, as distinguished from other games and contests, always includes an important component of physical as well as intellectual skill. Chess, according to this squint, is a contest, not a sport. This definition is not without some messy borderlines. There can be endless discussion as to whether auto and horse racing, for instance, are true sports. Is the contest between motorized vehicles or drivers? Between horses or jockeys? But the distinction is basic.

Participation in sport requires commitment and focus. The athlete must throw herself into the contest with abandon: "You got to have heart." At the same time there must be focus—mindfulness. Chicago Bulls basketball coach Phil Jackson (now coaching the L.A. Lakers), who approaches his sport from the perspective of Zen and American Indian spiritual disciplines, wants his players "to experience each moment with a clear mind and open heart." I take Jackson to mean commitment to, and focus on, the game. Religion in sport, be it individual or collective in expression, is meant to inspire total effort and mindful concentration—to "being in the moment."

I'll spare you an account of the deals I used to try to cut with God when, as a schoolboy, I stood in front of the goal posts just before the whistle blew for the opening kick-off. More current is the experience I had a few days ago when I was trying to decide whether to go through with a planned 10.6-mile day hike.

The guide book describes the section as containing "some of the longest climbs and highest peaks of any Georgia section" of the Appalachian Trail. I didn't want to do it for some fairly prudential reasons. But it was scheduled, as we say. Never mind whether trail hiking is true sport. It's physical, it's tiring and, on this section, once you start there's no turning back and no exit until the end. I needed to be attentive to commitment and to a quiet mind. Hiking also can have a spiritual dimension. I felt better, if also a bit lame, just for doing it.

Today the FSU football team will have a devotional session before the game. The objectives will be to inspire the players to be up for a total effort and to play with clear minds. Not so much "thinking" as mindfully doing well what they have learned to do in practice—except, this time, amid the noise, intimidation and chaos of the Swamp.

—February 20, 1999

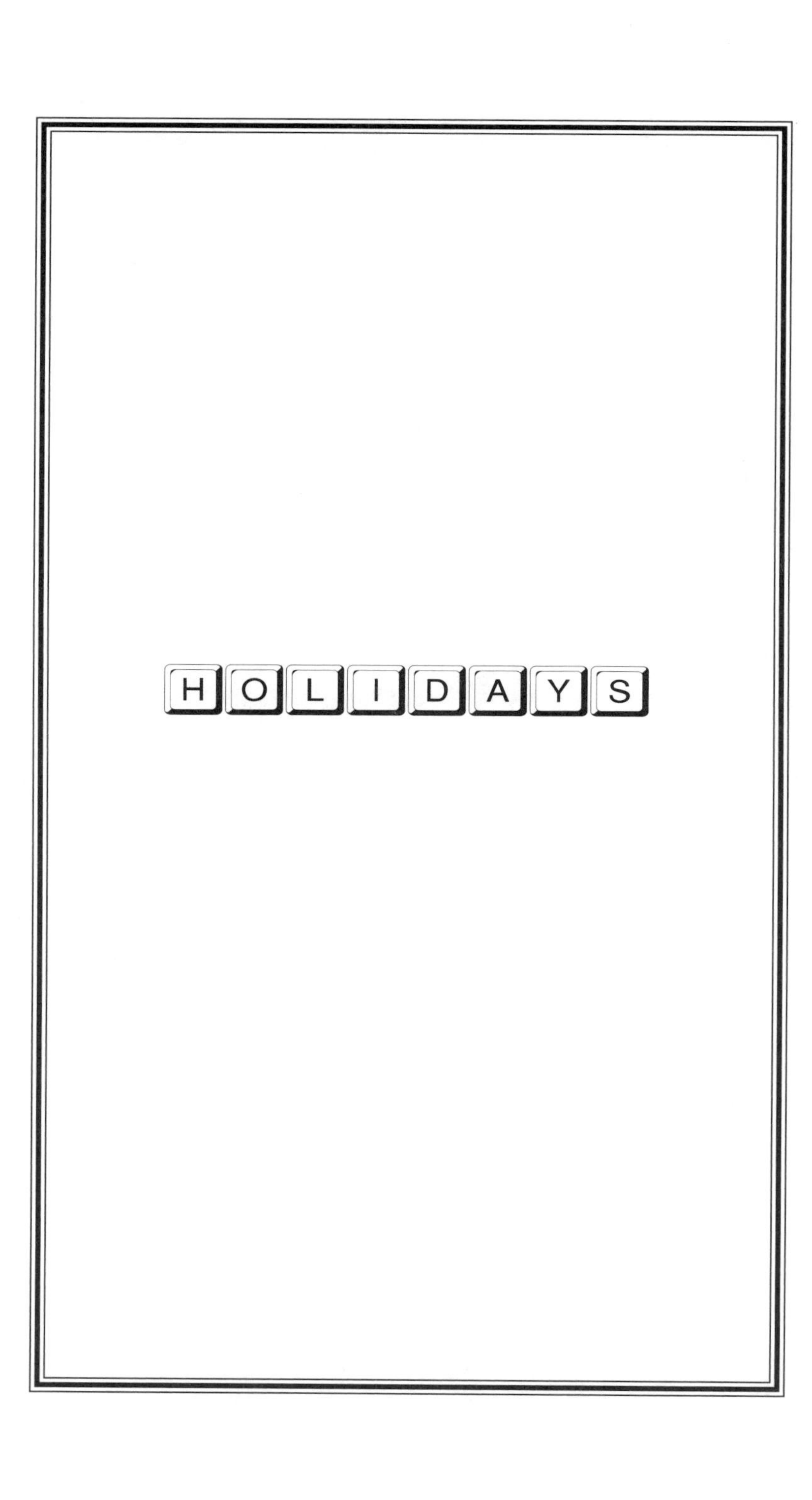
HOLIDAYS

Holidays

Selecting pieces on holidays—holy days—proved difficult. Choosing the three below necessitated the exclusion of columns on civil religious holidays—Memorial Day, the Fourth of July, and Thanksgiving—as well as such days as Halloween and more marginal observances. It also eliminated essays on the influence of the Exodus narrative in Western history, and thus of the centrality of Passover themes in Judaism and Christianity.

The first essay, "Thoughts on time, space, religion and she-crab soup," really is a discussion of the role of tradition in postmodernity. This is a theme to which I returned in both scholarly and popular writing. I guess I can write with more sophistication and precision on the subject today than I did in 1986, but I still believe what I wrote then is true and perhaps worth repeating.. One result of this column was my identification as a maker, and even something of a connoisseur of, she-crab soup.

The second selection, "King honored for impact on past, present, future," was written in defense of the establishment of a national holiday on King's birthday. There were a number of persons who weren't that enthusiastic about the action. One colleague told me that the column convinced him of the appropriateness of a King holiday, an outcome I don't often enjoy in my professional conversations.

The third, "The focus should be liturgy, not sermons, at high holy day services," reflects a long-standing conviction of mine as one who has been on both sides of the altar rail during major festival services. It is indeed a temptation for the preacher to prepare *the* sermon, the definitive tour de force that the occasion demands. The temptation should be resisted.

"Thoughts on taking time seriously," the fourth selection, was published on 1 January 2000. I wrote several "New Years" columns over fifteen years. For the premodern religious person—*homo* religiosis—the New Year's observance was the central festival. In ancient societies it was observed as a profoundly religious celebration. One of my repeated themes is that bringing the passage of time to mind creates anxieties for we who deal from the postmodern condition similar to those experienced by our premodern forebears. A related theme I emphasized more than once is the familiar admonition of most religions for us to remember life's brevity.

But when a columnist publishes a religious essay on the day of the generally perceived juncture of years, centuries, and millennia he is working with an embarrassment of riches! I wasn't tempted to summarize any (much less all) of the three periods. We had enough of that. While incorporating in passing the two themes mentioned above, I went for the whole nine yards and wrote of the relation between human consciousness and the concept of time itself. It is from the human necessity to "order" time, as arbitrary and superficial as the enterprise may be, that religious consciousness links the past (faith), present (love), and future (hope) by fashioning bonds of meaning.

Thoughts on time, space, religion, and she-crab soup

"We are reformers spring and summer; in autumn and winter we stand by the old; reformers in the morning, conservers at night." —Emerson

We have entered the season when tradition serves us better than innovation, ritual better than experiment. Tradition, in the most elementary sense of the word, is anything transmitted or handed down from the past. Tradition saves us from "the crush of mater and time," providing the basis for a sense of place and remembered history. In "Fiddler on the Roof," Tevye the dairyman, in speaking of his people, says, "One thing holds them together, makes them a community—tradition!"

Tradition is not necessarily based on rational deliberation. The "truth" of a tradition may or may not be based on acceptable evidence or accurate knowledge. Created through human thought and imagination, it is handed down from one generation to the next.

In 336 C.E., the practice of observing Dec.25 as the birthday of Christ was established in Rome, even though the date rests on neither historical foundation nor early church tradition. Most scholars agree the motive was the desire of the Roman Church to establish a Christina festival to rival the pagan celebration of the winter solstice (observed in the fourth century on Dec. 25).

The most ancient prayer of the Christ mass suggests the connection in the mind of the church between Christmas and the pagan observance: "O God, who hast made this most holy night to shine with the illumination of the true light..."

The Jewish observance of Hanukkah, the Festival of Lights, also occurs near the winter solstice. In a sense, Christianity and Judaism transformed an older tradition to proclaim an affirmation when the days are shortest: "The light has shined in the darkness and the darkness has not overcome it." This confession is the handed-down wisdom of the race.

In each household, certain traditions also mark the holidays. Thanksgiving in our house, for instance, is shared with the students and friends, but Christmas mostly with family. Turkey on Thanksgiving, but a goose on Christmas. My she-crab soup is seldom served other than on winter holidays. My wife's New England Indian pudding is for Thanksgiving alone. We light Advent candles. We decorate later and keep the tree up longer than most folks we know. Midnight service on Christmas Eve; gift exchange Christmas morning. This is the way it goes here.

Of course, there are more important traditions than holiday dishes that comprise a family legacy (although knowing how to make she-crab soup is one measure of excellence), but it is the little traditions that strengthen the social bond, both in families and among friends. On the larger scale, there are those core values a family must incorporate if its offspring are to have senses of self, place and heritage. The combination of central and peripheral traditions gives parents and children a sense of family.

Americans have tended to undervalue the past, emphasizing new experience over tradition. We are chronological snobs operating from a bias for the most recent event, the latest news. The new model is always assumed to be superior to the older one, the new learning preferred to the received truth.

In an important essay, "The American People, Their Space, Time, and Religion," church historian Sidney Mead maintained that movement through space rather than through time is the formative reality for Americans: "The American always believed...that he could, if he wished, move on in space and could even ignore the traditional boundaries of habit, class, custom, and law and begin anew, unfettered by these ancient restraints."

Americans have always had a sense of space, but not always a sense of place. The American has been the uprooted emigrant and immigrant, moving rapidly through space and always short on time. The Protestant revival hymn "Higher Ground" reflects both American religion and wider culture:

"I'm pressing on the upward way,
New Heights I'm gaining every day.
Still shouting as I onward bound,
Lord, plant my feet on higher ground."

Americans have indeed taken space more seriously than time, but it takes time, structured by tradition, to convert homogeneous space into a sense of place.

So what am I saying? Three cheers for tradition(s)? Well, yeah. I want to say a word for the role of tradition in human life, but I speak for tradition*ality*, not tradition*ism*, as one who believes that tradition has a place, but not as a tradition*ist*. To contrast the notion of static tradition with that of dynamic change is to miss the point: Tradition itself develops, and no innovation occurs without the support of tradition that gives it substance.

Tradition and change are in creative tension. The wisdom lies in achieving the correct mix. We should all, like St. Matthew's kingdom scribe, bring from our households "both that which is old and that which is new." Americans especially need to be reminded to settle down and settle in a bit. To take time to savor the season(s).

Emerson speaks of the tension between tradition and change as different phases of the natural cycle. Fall and Winter (the same season in North Florida) are the seasons to "stand by the old," or at least to lean a little in that direction.

—December 6, 1986

King honored for impact on past, present, future

This month, for the first time, the nation will observe a holiday honoring Martin Luther King Jr. Many feel a holiday is long overdue for King, whom I first met in 1957 and whose influence on my life was profound. Others are not persuaded that public and private offices should close in observance of King's person and work.

Here begins what for some is a reminder, and for others an argument, that our newest national holiday is in fact appropriate. It is justified because King has become a legend, transcending the particular achievements of his own life and times; because King was the last black leader who effectively united "black and white together" in behalf of racial justice in America; and because the concrete accomplishments of the movement he led made a real difference in American life.

King is a hero of legendary proportions. At an academic conference in 1984, I listened to a young scholar read a paper that initially annoyed me because I felt he was inaccurate about certain influences in King's social and intellectual background. Then it dawned on me that he was speaking not so much about the "Martin of history" as about the "King of legend." I was listening on one level; he was writing and speaking on another. His re-visioning of the meaning of the "King event" was quite legitimate.

In meaning and imagination, King indeed has become larger than life. We canonize those who inspire us to move ahead for a better world. Even in his lifetime, King had become such a symbol of the movement that he, at times, found the burden of the role almost unbearable.

His fusion of black and white America in that movement was crucial. Since the composition of the American population has been black and white, such a fusion is a requirement for any real solution to the problem of American racism. Swedish sociologist Gunnar Myrdal characterized the problem as an "American dilemma": the disparity between the "creed" of equality and the unequal status of African Americans.

Slaves were brought to Colonial America in 1619, but the black experience was not reflected in the original documents of the American civil religion. Just as the Puritans excluded the American Indians from "God's covenant with New England," so the Jeffersonians compromised on the inclusion of slaves as "men created equal" (And they quite probably did not intend that women be included either).

King's dream was, to a large extent, the American Dream. He was a unique blend of black Baptist preacher, social-gospel prophet and scholar/theologian, with an earned doctorate in systematic theology. His oratory was moving.

King's inclusion in the civil calendar of saints should be interpreted as the symbolic integration of the African American experience into the authorized version of the American story. His legacy is more than symbolic. Millions of black Americans, particularly in the South, vote today as a result of the Voting Rights Act of 1965. There are 6,056 black elected officials in America. A less quantifiable but perhaps more important legacy has been, in the words of the poet Robert E. Hayden, "the lives grown out of his life, the lives fleshing his dream of the beautiful, needful thing."

National responses to the American dilemma have occurred dramatically in approximately hundred-year cycles. Now, well more than 300 years after the first black slaves were brought to Jamestown, about 200 years since the Declaration of Independence and the Constitution, and more than 100 years after the Emancipation Proclamation, it is appropriate that the grandson of former slaves be included with slave-owning Virginia planters, and the Illinois railroad lawyer in the official pantheon of American heroes.

—January 4, 1986

Ministers should focus on liturgy, not sermon, during Easter services

Reinhold Niebuhr, the Protestant theologian who was a self-conscious nonconformist, said that, on Christmas and Easter, he preferred "a liturgical church with as little sermon as possible." Niebuhr felt that the important events—stories—of a religious tradition (in his case, Christianity) are more akin to great poetry than rational analysis, and that "there are not many poets in the pulpit." Too often, Niebuhr believed, sermons on the big days tend to defend the validity of the events and to establish their acceptability to the modern intellect. Niebuhr concluded that "symbolic presentation of the poetry in hymn, anthem, and liturgy" is preferable to much explanation.

I agree with Niebuhr, at least as it applies to Holy Week and Easter observances. Perhaps the Passover Seder has something of a seminar motif and Niebuhr's remarks may apply more to Rosh Hashana and Yom Kippur in the Jewish experience. But when it comes to the experience of Holy Week and, particularly, Easter Sunday I would just as soon avoid disquisitions on the differences between the idea of the resurrection of the body and the notion of the immortality of the soul.

I recall being assaulted (that's how I felt) one Easter service by the argument for the immortality of the soul buttressed by Wernher von Braun's belief in it. Wernher von Braun, yet. I suppose that one accepts von Braun's authority in rocket science and his belated service in behalf of democratic causes, but he was neither then nor now my mentor in faith and ethics. What should I think if von Braun did not believe in the immortality of the soul?

Then there are mindless sermonettes about lilies and tulips, which even the less than gifted child knows are really about reproduction, not resurrection. In our part of the world, nature often provides a luxurious context for Passover and Lenten-Easter observances. But the stories are about liberation from bondage and news from a graveyard, not Springtime Tallahassee with hymns. For some of us nature worship is tempting enough without the church confusing it with *the* story.

I am not engaging in priest and pastor bashing. In my own pastoral experience I am certain that congregations suffered through my efforts to say it all. I know the mixed feelings that clergy often experience as they confront Easter and Christmas crowds. The pressure to rise to the occasion, the letdown after the festival. That is precisely why it is probably wise to put more of the celebration on automatic pilot and to let the poets and musicians take over.

It is hard to improve on the readings of the Passion from Matthew's Gospel that begin the Holy Week commemoration on Palm Sunday. Christians have known this since the fourth century when the procession into Jerusalem was reenacted. Good Friday needs little homiletical intervention or embellishment other than commemoration and meditation. A matter of sacred texts, music, and liturgy, by and large. When the creeds are sung Niebuhr writes that the "alchemy of the service has changed what was once poetry and has been made into dogma back into poetry again."

When the boy soprano at Kings College Chapel intones the first notes of "Once in David's Royal City" on Christmas Eve, it is unnecessary, even intrusive, to hear a bishop discourse on the incarnation. Something at once both particular and universal stirs my heart when my favorite soprano sings John of Damascus'

> *Come, ye faithful, raise the strain*
> *Of triumphant gladness;*
> *God has brought his Israel*
> *Into joy from sadness;*
> *Loosed from Pharaoh's bitter yoke,*
> *Jacob's sons and daughters;*
> *Led them with unmoistened foot*
> *Through the Red Sea waters.*

I don't need von Braun's speculation on the immortality of the soul to augment it.

—April 11, 1992

Thoughts on taking time seriously

Now that we have crossed into the new year-century-millennium it is natural and probably necessary to stop and catch our breath. We know that the borders marking these periods are arbitrary and inexact. Yet we also know that what we are experiencing is not merely superstition, but designations that carry profound symbolic force.

Today the big round zeros transform our diaries and our calendars. We are both blessed and cursed with the rare opportunity to witness and experience all three transitions. Blessed because it is indeed a special occasion that not many who come before and after us share; cursed because it is difficult enough to handle the turning of one year or even a century, but thinking about all three dispensations gets very heavy.

Our musings are shot through with confusion. We mix millennial and centenarian reflections. Even the *New York Times* devotes "Reflections on the Millennium" essays to what really turn out to be reviews of the 20th century. It is difficult enough to sort through a year's events, more demanding to indulge *fin-de-siecle* considerations at century's end, and an awesome challenge to do the millennium justice.

And the uneasiness we experience is pretty much global now that the Gregorian calendar—the Common Era calendar—has been adopted by the United Nations.
What lies at the bottom of our preoccupation with decades, centuries and millennia is our common need to take time seriously. Experiencing divisions in time may be encoded into human beings. We seem driven to order time as a way of creating meaning in life.

Religion has played a crucial role in delineating particular days, cycles of the year, or "events" (even though they may be inexact or mythical) as special—holy—in a community's experience. In fact such delineations create our religious communities.

We are also a death-haunted species. As individuals we come to realize that we are not only in time, but that time is in us. Our personal pilgrimage ends in death. An important function of religion is to enable us to deal with mortality: "So teach us to number (count) our days…memento mori." This is why melancholy often settles over our spirits as we note those who have died and as we contemplate our own deaths when we mark the passing of the years.

So what are we dealing with today perhaps is milestone overload. What I guess we need to do is take our time taking time seriously, so to speak. The Roman Catholic Church, which takes calendric millennialism very seriously, is observing Holy Year 2000, a Jubilee celebration lasting throughout the year. We don't have a Jan 1 deadline for things to have to come together. It takes time to get a perspective on a given year or century.

We can deal with the tradition(s) of our religious faith emphasizing patterns in history that make sense of our experience. This is the foundation for faith. From this we have a basis for a hope that promises a usable future. For the time being we can provide continuity between past and future by continuing to focus on our everyday responsibilities. The millennium is a human construct and nothing cataclysmic happened at midnight. In the meantime life goes on. Until it doesn't.

The world will not end. Until it does.

—January1, 2000

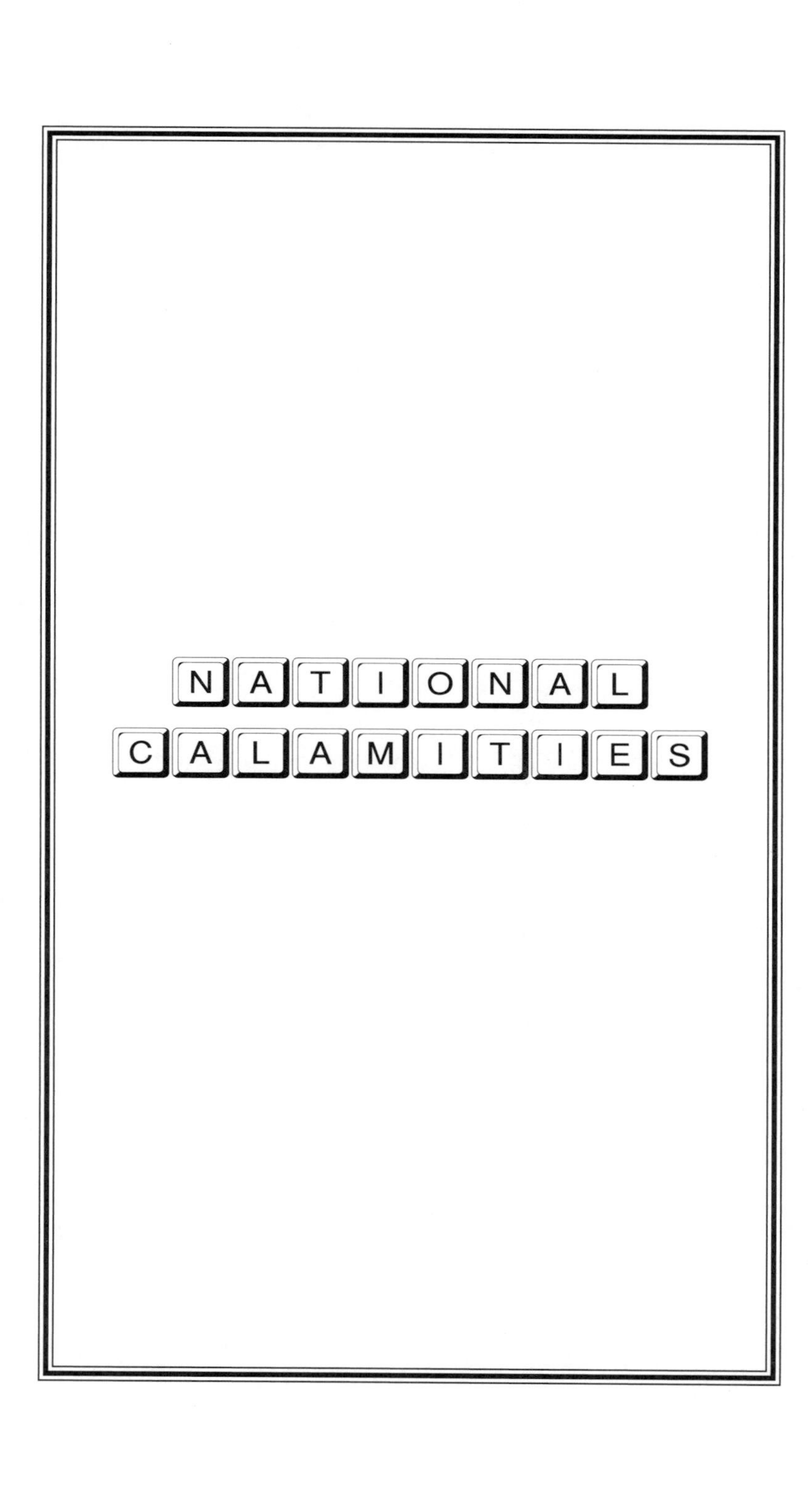
NATIONAL
CALAMITIES

National Calamities

Selections from columns dealing with national calamities include one on the Challenger space shuttle explosion, two on the Waco conflagration and Oklahoma City bombing, one on the Littleton Colorado school massacre, and finally my comment on the attacks on the World Trade Center and the Pentagon September 11, 2001.

"Grief for national heroes assuaged by civil religious observance" was commentary on the way in which the American civil religion was effectively expressed by President Ronald Reagan at the national memorial service for the Challenger crew. Reagan's experience as an actor was excellent background for one component of the presidential role: presiding in times of national crisis. He was perhaps the only president who knew precisely how he appeared on camera and how to play an assigned role. I wrote that the high priest of the civil religion is the president. I also spoke of James Reston, at the time the most influential columnist in American journalism, as a prophet of the civil religion, one who speaks truth to power from the standpoint of the national covenant. The column was also the occasion for describing civil religion in America.

"Religious cults, Waco Texas and finger pointing," is representative of several opinions I published, most of them as regular columns for the *Tallahassee Democrat*, in which I was critical of the Justice Department's handling of Waco and its self-serving investigations and interpretations of the event. The column, "Remembering both Waco and Oklahoma City" was an inadequate attempt to conflate the two events in one piece. It was mostly about Waco. I was called by several media representatives asking my opinion before I had even heard about the Oklahoma City bombing. Reporters were wondering if I thought there was linkage between Waco and Oklahoma City and if the bombers were probably Middle-East terrorists. It turned out the answers were yes and no. In the minds of the bombers, at least, there was a relation between the two events. But the answer to the second question was no. We learned that terrorist violence is not always a "foreign" import. We have a domestic variety which can be just as fanatical and deadly.

"Living through the questions after Littleton" engaged the way we dealt with the massacre at Columbine High in Littleton Colorado. My point in this column is that perhaps more important than the question of evil and undeserved suffering, is the question of whether we can endure and prevail in the wake of such an event. Perhaps what religious faith and worship assures us is that we "can live through the questions without knowing all the answers."

"After prayers comes repentance" was written in the wake of the attacks on the World Trade towers and the Pentagon. It was the first time in over sixteen years that my editor worried over my possibly getting clobbered by readers who might perceive me as being unpatriotic and blaming the United States for causing the horrible crime by my using the word "repentance." Apparently most readers also thought we should be repenting, although I suspect fewer would agree with me regarding the three attitudes I suggest we abandon after 9:11:01.

Grief for national heroes rooted in civil religion

The day after the space shuttle exploded, one of my students came by the office and said, "All I can think of is American civil religion, Professor. We are seeing civil religion in its most powerful expression."

The student, a biochemistry major who had taken my course, "Religion in America" the semester before, was correct. Our national grieving for the Challenger heroes is probably the most intense expression of the American civil religion since the assassination of John F. Kennedy. Civil religion is a faith that exists alongside the religion of our churches and synagogues. This "Religion of the Republic" is not an unquestioned devotion to the national government, but rather a strong commitment to its founding principles.

It is seen most clearly in the religious interpretation of the nation's secular history. America has portrayed its mission in divine terms: God oversees American destiny and approves of its founding values. It draws from biblical sources and Western history, but it is neither distinctly Christian nor Jewish. Political sovereignty rests with the people, but ultimate sovereignty is attributed to God: "In God We Trust."

The American civil religion has its own elaborate rituals. Its scriptures include the foundation documents of the nation and other important writings—the Gettysburg Address, Lincoln's Second Inaugural. Its holy days include the Fourth of July and Thanksgiving. Its sacred places include Arlington National Cemetery and Valley Forge. Its saints are the national heroes. Its ceremonies include presidential inaugurations and the recent memorial services for "our Challenger heroes."

Most nations attribute a sacred character to their national experience, but we Americans have self-consciously assigned a religious meaning to our very conception. The late G.K. Chesterton wrote, "America is the only nation in the world that is founded on a creed. That creed is set forth with dogmatic and even theological lucidity in the Declaration of Independence." Sidney Mead, an American religious historian, wrote, "America is a nation with the soul of a church."

The high priest of our civil religion is the president. President Reagan is a superb liturgist for civil-religious ritual, perhaps the best we have had. He offered the eulogy at the Challenger memorial services January 31: "The nation...will long feel the loss of her seven sons and daughters, her seven good friends. We can find consolation only in faith, for we know in our hearts that you who flew so high and so proud now make your home beyond the stars, safe in God's promise of eternal life."

Our connection of religion with society can create a consensus on important values, which are derived from a point of reference that transcends the nation. Without it, Lincoln's appeal to mutual forgiveness after the Civil War would not have made sense. Without it, Martin Luther King's movement would have completely failed. Ours is a nation founded to establish a secular version of the New Israel, the chosen people with "a manifest destiny" under God. This can lead to identifying the national interest with the divine will. A nation on such a mission is likely to shout, "Get out of our way!" Such a perspective can all too easily avoid self-criticism.

But, the civil religion also has prophets and some of its prophets are beginning to criticize aspects of the space program. James Reston asked in his column, "Where are we going?" As he pondered the meaning of the shuttle tragedy and applied it to Reagan's Strategic Defense Initiative, or "Star Wars," Reston asked, even if this plan worked 96 percent of the time, would not the "four percent of missiles that get through destroy the Republic as we know it?"

Certainly the shuttle tragedy is a judgment on an extreme technological pride that assumes total control over nature and the near perfection of human engineering. The space disaster also appropriately recalls the "unsinkable Titanic." American know-how is, alas, finite and imperfect. The space program has been the jewel in our national crown for 25 years. Despite assassinations, Vietnam, Watergate and the Iranian hostage crisis, the space program gave the nation success and patriotic pride. The disaster could be the occasion for a crisis in national confidence.

As the bruised American psyche recovers, the resources of our civil religion are providing consolation, grief therapy, and even critical reflection.

—February 15, 1986

Religious cults, Waco, Texas, and finger-pointing

I am neither a Clinton basher nor a Janet Reno critic, but count me among those who feel that the Bureau of Alcohol, Tobacco, and Firearms and the FBI botched the showdown with David Koresh. The responsibility, finally, rests with the President and the Attorney General. I agree that Reno is to be commended for being unhesitatingly up front regarding her responsibility, Clinton less so for his belated acceptance of responsibility. Both the President and White House spokesman George Stephanopoulos were less than forthcoming, initially scapegoating by saying "it's a decision by the Attorney General."

I disagree, however, with the *Tallahassee Democrat* editorial board's opinion that the Waco tragedy is "not of the FBI's making." It is not entirely of the Bureau's making, of course, but neither was it inevitable that things ended as they did. Had the feds been less concerned with ending the siege and more in tune with the nature of religious cults and their leadership, the conflagration might have been avoided. There is little doubt that the astringent light of critical analysis already begun will continue to expose governmental clumsiness, contradictory rationale and self-serving interpretations of what happened.

One does not have to be high on David Koresh and his followers to suggest that they were the objects of assault in the first place with an eye to publicity for the ATF. Secondly, they were victims of impatience on the part of the FBI. The continued reference to members of the compound as hostages, finally, signals a fundamental misunderstanding. Members of a high-intensity religious commune who have separated themselves from establishment society are not really hostages in the conventional sense of the term. For the FBI and its advisors to employ typical hostage liberation strategies and tactics was to miss the mark.

One doesn't have to be remarkably intelligent, moreover, to question whether frontal assault is the fitting approach to a group that is informed by apocalyptic adventism and watching for an imminent climax to history in terms of fire and warfare.

Koresh possibly was a psychopath. Again, one doesn't deal with psychopaths by cornering them and, through "systematically reducing their options," giving them no way out that saves them from humiliation.

I find it surprising that the managers of Monday's attack were surprised with the cult's response. If the decision makers did not factor into their analysis the possibility of collective suicide or violent response, they were, as it turned out, fatally naïve. The *Democrat* editorial writer admonished readers that, "the finger-pointing we can do without." One person's "finger-pointing" is another's citizen's alert. At any rate, accountability we cannot do without. It should be pointed out that, bottom line, the Waco tragedy illustrates the inability of secular government officials to take Koresh seriously as one who believed his own message. He didn't have to be the Messiah to mean what he said. So we had opposing sides that spoke past each other in an escalating contest of wills.

Perhaps the greatest danger in responding to marginal religious groups is overreaction. If such communities violate laws they should be prosecuted. If we believe in religious liberty, we refrain from persecuting them on the basis of their peculiar beliefs or bizarre behavior (unless, of course, their behavior threatens the welfare of others). Liberty is an instrumental value; its exercise guarantees neither saving truth nor excellent behavior. Religious freedom is often inconvenient, and its exercise time-consuming.

We probably pushed too fast in Waco. America usually has space enough to accommodate the religiously bizarre. In Waco we just didn't feel we had the time.

—April 24 1993

Remembering both Waco and Oklahoma City

Note two melancholy anniversaries that occurred Monday: the sixth anniversary of the Waco conflagration and the fourth anniversary of the Oklahoma City bombing. This may sound like yesterday's news, but we still have work to do on these two stories.

While folks in Oklahoma City observed the anniversary in quiet ceremony, PBS's "Frontline" aired "Waco: The

Inside Story." April 19 certainly is an important date for members of the far, far right. On that date in 1775, the first shots of the Revolutionary War were fired in Concord, Mass. On that date in 1995, Arkansas extremist Richard Wayne Snell was executed for the murder of a supposedly Jewish Texarkana pawnbroker.

We can dismiss the stringing together of these anniversaries as important only to paranoid curators of such a calendar. But remember that prosecutors in the Timothy McVeigh and Terry Nichols cases maintained that their motive for the Oklahoma City bombing was revenge for the federal raid on the Branch Davidian compound near Waco. That makes it important for all of us.

The feds botched the Branch Davidian "problem" from start to finish. The Bureau of Alcohol, Tobacco, and Firearms could have investigated and charged the Davidians with illegally stockpiling weapons without the bloody invasion of the compound, an invasion that constituted an hour-long gunfight. The bureau lost the shoot-out and brought on a 51-day standoff.

The FBI pursued a "good cop/bad cop" strategy by alternating between its Hostage Rescue Team and its Negotiating Command Post. There was significant tension between the two, and poor communication. Both lobbied the attorney general, pushing their approaches. The trouble was that the negotiators could not begin to understand Davidian leader David Koresh's biblical apocalyptic mindset. They grew impatient with his theology and his stubbornness. Their tactics simply strengthened the Davidians' cohesion, compressing them into a tighter community.

It is understandable that alienated government haters would recoil at photos of M-60 tanks inserting—poking—CS gas into the compound's main house. The wider culture showed little empathy (let alone sympathy) for the

Davidians. Media coverage tended to focus on "the cult problem." Most talk shows followed the position that people in "cults" are totally manipulated even though they usually don't realize it. Most print and electronic journalism accentuated the spectacular and bizarre.

Our general policy toward groups such as the Branch Davidians should be one of reasonable permissiveness. If they violate civil or criminal codes, we should of course prosecute. But we should not prosecute them for strange ideology or communal lifestyles. Heresy or strangeness is not a felony in the United States. Heresy can hardly be a serious vice in a culture in which no particular orthodoxy is an esteemed virtue.

We err when we respond too powerfully and too impatiently to such groups. The danger is that we will drive more of our brothers and sisters who have adopted the religion of alienation to the more extreme religion (and politics) of total paranoia.

At Waco we didn't run out of time. We ran out of patience.

—April 24, 1999

Living through the questions after Littleton

Much of the commentary on the Littleton massacre, although at times insightful and even inspiring, has been unfocused and diffuse. That is understandable. There are so many aspects to Littleton that one can go off in many directions. Probing the many "why" questions is an exercise steeped in complexity.

I'll spare you my opinions on video games, the Net, media coverage of the event, gun control, jocks and nerds, goths and normals, Marilyn Manson, and our collective recollection of the dark side of high school. I'll bypass comment on "the toxic culture of guns and screen violence that kids have to navigate" to which Tipper Gore refers in her *Time* essay. My focus is to note the role religious groups played in this gruesome story.

Religion is the way we give meaning to our lives through a more or less integrated system of beliefs and practices. But religion also is the way in which groups and individuals deal with the ultimate questions. On the first Sunday after the Littleton rampage pews were crowded nationwide with worshipers who were seeking answers with an unusual sense of urgency. Ministers and Rabbis provided a number of answers to questions raised by such wanton human evil. The Rev. Susan Swanson of Luther Memorial Church in Chicago advised: "Take off the earphones, turn off the TV, turn down the radio...Start speaking words of love and kindness in our families." Rabbi Ronald M. Shapiro of Congregation Shalom, in Fox Point, Wis., similarly remarked that "the preciousness of human life" can be lost in the pace of American life. Boston Roman Catholic Cardinal Bernard Law said that in the U.S. "guns are too accessible and too acceptable."

I think New York City's Cardinal John O'Connor spoke to the most pressing question in St. Patrick's Cathedral when he prayed for those "emotionally and spiritually shattered" by the killings. The ultimate question in the face of such emotional cataclysm is "Can we get through this? Can we go on?"

Think about how emotionally and spiritually shattering it is. In our society those institutions which generate the most intense sense of community are schools and religious congregations. And the school, Columbine High, was the target. The school: schoolmates and teachers!

In Littleton the churches were the center for most of the gatherings during the week. They provided the occasion for a shattered community coming together again. The last service in a week of funerals was for Isaiah Shoels, a 4-foot, 11-inch black football player. As many as 5,000 persons—dignitaries and common folk—came to the Heritage Christian Center to celebrate the life, not only of Shoels, but the lives of all 13 victims of the Colorado shooting. "This is the last piece, now the healing begins," said the Rev. Larry Russell, one of the pastors at Heritage. After the two-and-a half hour service and after Isaiah's casket had been closed, another pastor, the Rev. Dennis Leonard, called those remaining in the congregation down to the altar. The pastor asked them to lift their right hand and say, "Isaiah's life was not in vain." They said it and then they clapped and cheered.

The choir started singing, "It'll be all right," and people began dancing in the aisles. Some were even smiling when they filed out, reassured that it'll be all right. Perhaps the assurance is that one can live through the questions without knowing all the answers.

—May 8, 1999

After prayers come repentance

In the wake of the attacks, religious faith and worship provided solace for our sorrow; community for our sense of isolation; and expressions of unified resolve for our fear and distress. From spontaneous gatherings to denominational services to civil religious observances, our turn to church, mosque, synagogue, temple and street meetings for healing demonstrated the pious component of American life.

The September 14 memorial service in Washington's National Cathedral on the Day of Mourning was a most tasteful, inclusive and effective expression of the American Civil Religion 2001. Billy Graham's thoughtful remarks and Denyce Graves' singing of "America the Beautiful" combined realistic comfort with powerful emotion. President Bush's comments probably were his most balanced and eloquent in those first days after the attacks.

Even as the healing and memorialization continue, it is time now to think of another religious response required for the living of these days: repentance. Biblically, the generic meaning of "repentance" is turning away from sin and back to God. It has the secondary and tertiary meanings of a sense of regret or remorse, and a simple change of mind. But the fully developed and primary biblical meaning is that of a reorientation of an individual's or community's whole life, requiring the adoption of a new ethical line of conduct.

To repent literally means to "turn around." We have some turning—repenting—to do if we are going to engage this new condition "in which things will never be the same again." We need to repent some of the attitudes and actions that have characterized our nation for, in some cases, as long as the past two decades.

Please note that by the idea of repentance, I imply neither that we brought the attacks on ourselves nor that God is punishing us for our sins. Rather, I am suggesting disciplines that we need as we respond to Bush's call to patience and resolution.

First, we need to turn from our recent anti-government ideology and the denigration of public service. Deregulation of the airlines and security measures provided by the airlines hardly have proved successful. A number of airlines now will survive only be great transfusions from the public treasury. When our heroes are firefighters and police officers, politicians' posturing against government, suggesting that privatization is the answer to all problems, is plainly wrong. It has been irresponsible; to continue it now would be obscene.

Second, we need to turn from the politics of pandering and ask our leaders "to talk sense to the American people." We don't need tax refunds as much as we need to be awakened from the false consciousness that we "can have it all." We need to abandon the Cold War theology of missile shields and massive retaliation for a smart, lean and mean call to the "high standards of strength and sacrifice" required of us in what appears to be the "long twilight struggle" in which we are now engaged. Bush got a promising start in this direction in his address to Congress Thursday night.

Third, we need to do a U-turn from the unilateral lane. Reaching out for friends is a reflexive action in this kind of tragedy. Since Sept. 11, we've suddenly realized how dependent we are upon allies, we who rejected the Kyoto Treaty, rejected the ABM treaty and walked out of the U.N. racism conference. We have been undependable in meeting our U.N. membership responsibilities.

Two points:

- The fact that we are the world's remaining super-power doesn't mean that we can reach our objectives alone.
- It is a form of barbarism in 2001 to leave the conference table and walk out. We can keep our own counsel and disagree fiercely with other nations, but choosing when and whether we will participate really is to choose not to participate.

Putting it constructively, we can say it no better than Abraham Lincoln's statement: "as our case is new, so we must think anew, and act anew. We must disenthrall ourselves, and then we shall save our country." But first, as we begin looking up from the smoke and ashes, we acknowledge that some normalcy is not worth returning to. We need, brothers and sisters, to repent.

—September 22, 2001

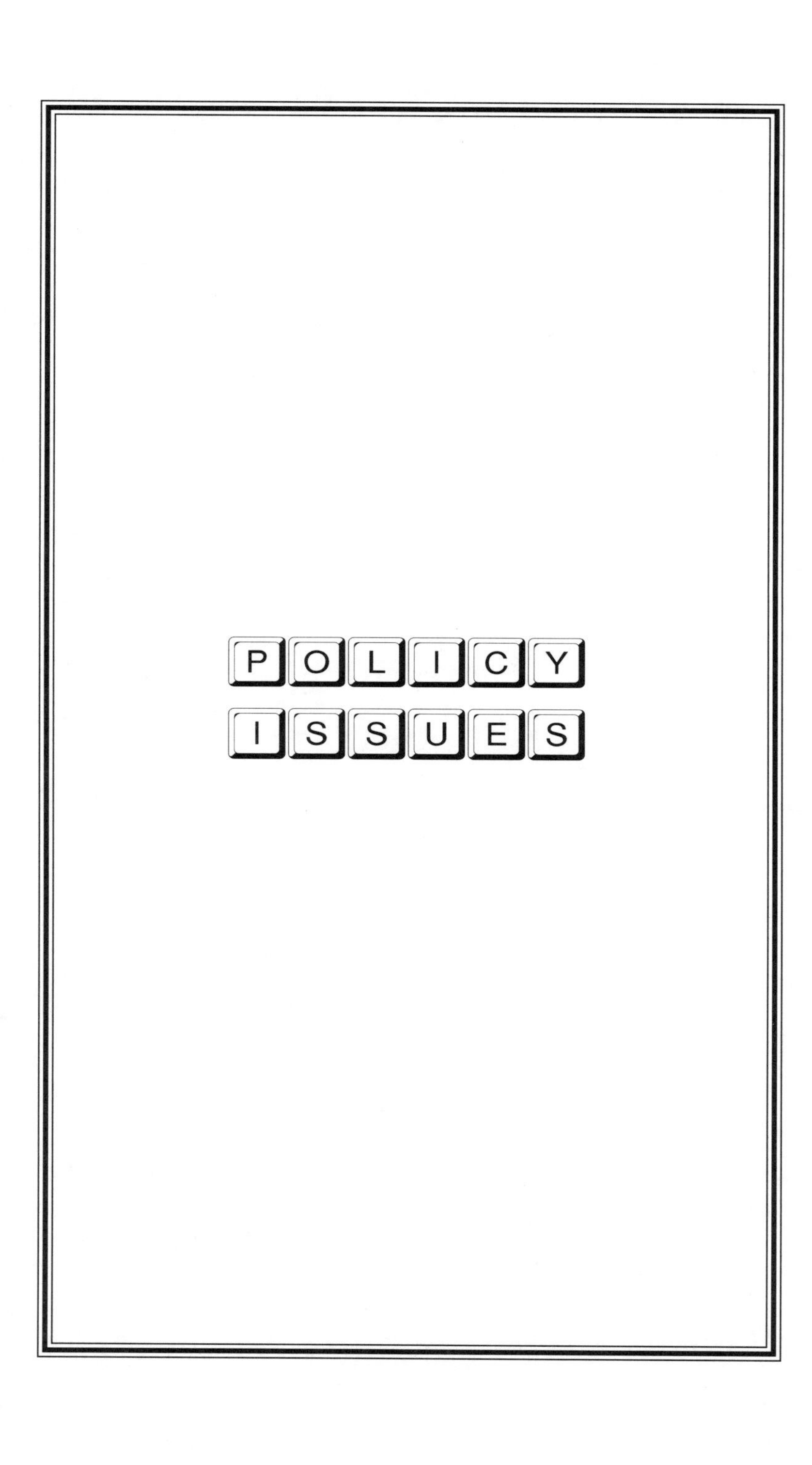
POLICY
ISSUES

Policy Issues

The ethical aspects of public policy issues have continually interested me. I was trained in seminaries and graduate schools by a number of faculty who were significantly influenced by the Social Gospel tradition, emphasizing the imperative of social reconstruction as an integral part of Christian commitment. My identification with Martin Luther King, Jr. and participation in the civil rights movement as a young adult contributed to an activist emphasis in my professional life. From 1974-1979 I was the founder and director of the Institute for Social Policy Studies, a center which attempted to bring together members of the academy, the Florida Legislature, and religious communities to deal with the moral dimensions of policy considerations.

"Time for religious groups to face the reality of AIDS" was my first column on the AIDS pandemic. My suggestions seem either obvious or dated (or both) now, but in 1987 there was still something of a conspiracy of silence that needed to be engaged.

Abortion was the major point of conflict in our society through the decades of the 1970s and the 1980s. It certainly had an impact on my life even before the Supreme Court's Roe decision in 1973. As a pastor and chaplain I was involved in problem-pregnancy counseling and I struggled for many years attempting to act responsibly and compassionately both in personal advice and public policy discussion. "An abortion consensus? Permit it but discourage it" is probably as representative of my position as any column I wrote on the issue. I am unequivocally pro-choice, but not untroubled by the reality of abortion.

"America's death penalty is still an issue" is one of the most recent of many columns on the death penalty. It is a bit satirical, but I hope not rude. The problem is that it is hard to be patient with folk who seem to be just now discovering problems that one has been concerned about for over three decades. Better late...

Over the years my opposition to capital punishment has increased. About abortion, I am troubled: about the death penalty I am clear and as certain as I ever get. I do allow that an argument in behalf of it for some very special cases is not unreasonable and I respect and talk with those who make it. But the death penalty aligns us with some of the most despotic nations and separates us from countries who share our human rights tradition. Capital punishment is an anachronism, a losing policy. Its perpetuation makes us losers in both our local and global communities.

I was and am not very supportive of President Bush's faith-based initiatives. I wrote an earlier column urging that we proceed with caution regarding the program. Now a number of "the devil is in the details" problems have emerged and the idea is in trouble. I hope that there will be a growing recognition that expanded government support for faith-based groups is apt to result in an unconstitutionally excessive entanglement between religious groups and the state. The selected column for this policy issue is my most recent one: "Faith-based ministries are just that." It is a more indirect and perhaps, therefore, a more positive argument, emphasizing the character of faith-based charities, than the dangers of government involvement. The selection provides the opportunity to celebrate one of my favorite faith-based ministries: Habitat for Humanity.

Time for religious groups to face the reality of AIDS

The AIDS epidemic is beginning to get the attention it deserves. Inasmuch as AIDS may be the most horrible plague in modern history, now spreading through the American population, it is high time we take it seriously. When it appeared that AIDS was primarily, if not exclusively the problem of socially disadvantaged groups, most of us could pass by on the other side of the road. Now that it is clear AIDS will affect everybody, societal stress is growing.

There is talk of mandatory testing and screening. Representatives for some religious groups have called for quarantining all suspected carriers of the AIDS virus—millions of people quarantined for life.

More measured responses are coming from leaders in science, medicine and education as they consider the economic, legal and human costs in this battle. The story of AIDS is getting increasing media coverage: "Data Shows AIDS Risk Widening." As usual the politicians—particularly the presidential candidates—are the slowest to respond. As an aide to one presidential candidate expressed it: "Everyone is trying to avoid this issue because it combines homosexuality, sexual disease and death, matters on which most of us wish to be unenlightened."

What can religious groups contribute to the battle against an enemy that could divide our increasingly fragmented society even more? They can participate by shunning moralistic interpretations, promoting moral responsibility and affirming the social virtues of compassion and inclusive community.

AIDS began its movement in America through three specific groups: homosexuals, Haitians, and those who share hypodermic needles. This was largely an accident of circumstance. In central Africa, where AIDS probably originated, the disease has spread largely through heterosexual activity. Those who maintain that AIDS is divine judgment against sexual immorality—and a number of religious leaders have done so—should consider that homosexual practice, heterosexual promiscuity and drug abuse have been going on for some time now.

There is also not much new about the epidemic spread of disease. What is new is a heretofore dormant natural virus that is now causing immense human suffering.

Those who interpret AIDS as God's punishment of sinners have to account for HIV infection in a newborn baby or in a woman infected by a bisexual husband. There are major theological problems with a doctrine that makes God directly responsible for the AIDS epidemic. Nor is the spread of this dread disease the appropriate occasion for condemning homosexuality. Gay-bashing is a form of scapegoating that skews our proper focus away from all high-risk sexual activity to that of sexual preference. This is no time for simplistic moralistic judgments; it is time, however, that we press the issue of genuine moral responsibility.

A morally responsible approach begins with a respect for the facts. AIDS therapy seems to be somewhat promising, but cure may never be possible. Mass immunization against the HIV virus is not a reasonable expectation in the near future. Education and sane public-health measures are the only feasible ways we now have of preventing its spread. Explicit sex education, therefore, should be carried out, especially in our schools. For those who will not practice abstinence and for the 40 percent of American adults who are unmarried, "safe sex" will have to be the norm. Those who are in a high-risk population for HIV infection and who refuse to have tests should assume they test positively. If they prefer wishful thinking to certainty, that is their right. It is not their right, however, to infect others.

Voluntary testing is a moral responsibility for those in high-risk groups who are going to be sexually active. Premarital testing is likewise in the best interests of both marital partners and of their unborn children. For those who are still in such a 1960s consciousness that they don't realize the "post-pill paradise" was never realized, it is time to wake up. Casual sex and promiscuity, like smoking and hard liquor, are passé. As it turns out, not every aspect of the "sexual revolution" was a success. Traditional values often are in place because they reflect the wisdom of the race over a sustained period of time.

The third contribution religious bodies can and should make to the human struggle against AIDS is the affirmation of inclusive community. One of the primary concerns of the major religious traditions is for a sense of *communitas*. In the face of this assault by a pandemic disease, we need to affirm our social solidarity.

AIDS victims have become the human equivalent of lepers in biblical times or perhaps of untouchables in the Hindu caste system. The biblical ethic of neighbor love requires that we reach out in compassion to those who experience the pain, physical disintegration, and almost certain death that HIV infection brings. That will involve provision for the adequate medical and personal needs of those who are afflicted, their families and friends. It will require the coordinated and concentrated efforts of government officials, educators, social-service professionals, clergy and counselors.

For far too long a small cadre of physicians, nurses and members of the gay community have waged the battle. They need our support.

—May 2, 1987

An abortion consensus? Permit it but discourage it

Both the prudent politician and the cautious columnist are wont to avoid the abortion thing. It is the obvious lose-lose topic of our day. Many people feel that, given the bitter polarization it arouses, thoughtful and fruitful discussion is impossible. Yet to avoid discussing the problem is to leave it to extremists who are engaging in civil warfare rather than civil argument.

I am commending a wise and lucid book which offers a helpful approach for "the great majority of Americans" who experience "deep ambivalence" about the resolution of the abortion problem. The book is, *Life Itself: Abortion in the American Mind*, written by Roger Rosenblatt and published this year by Random House.

Rosenblatt, currently editor-at-large for *Life*, has been an essayist and columnist for several major newspapers and journals. His book is a quite readable discussion that reviews American ambivalence on abortion, 4,000 years of abortion policy in all civilizations, aspects of the American character that shape our present attitudes, and a suggested resolution.

Rosenblatt states—correctly, in my opinion—that, "Most Americans are both for the choice of abortion as a principle and against abortion itself—for themselves. To state that ambivalence is to begin to deal with it." Polls do indeed seem to indicate that approximately 75% of the American people are in favor of abortion rights and approximately the same majority consider abortion as a "form of murder."

One sees the nation's ambiguity reflected in the candidates' attitudes. On the one hand, both Dan Quayle and George Bush have taken somewhat softer stands on abortion when the question is posed in personal, parental terms than the official Republican Party platform position. Bush, in answering what he would do if his granddaughter came to him and said she wanted to have an abortion, allowed that, after trying to make the case against it, the decision would be hers: "Who else's could it be?"

On the other hand, both Bill Clinton and Al Gore have shown signs of personal discomfort with abortion that suggest they are less than untroubled pro-choice advocates. The discomfort springs primarily from the fact that abortion touches on ultimate questions of human existence. That is, there is a religious dimension that quickly emerges. Most significant questions in life, if pushed far enough, end up being religious in nature. This certainly is true of abortion. Rosenblatt states it well: "Give abortion five seconds of thought, and it quickly spirals down in the mind to the most basic questions about human life, to the mysteries of birth and our relationship with our souls. It is difficult to disentangle, much less express, the feelings it engenders."

Religious groups participate in the nation's ongoing attempts to answer, "How are we to order our lives?" Answering that question probably is more difficult and painful these days than it has been for some time. In times of change and resulting uncertainty, it is perfectly legitimate for faith communities to contribute to what Walter Lippmann used to call "the public philosophy," but the pluralistic character of American life creates a severe curve in the movement from sectarian conviction to public policy.

The Reverend Richard McBrien of the theological faculty at the University of Notre Dame has said that Catholics have to respect the lack of consensus on the abortion question in our society. McBrien, who is religiously and personally opposed to abortion, nonetheless recognizes that personal morality in a democracy sometimes coincides with the majority opinion, sometimes not. What do we do if there is no consensus?

But isn't there an emerging consensus? Rosenblatt thinks so: "What most Americans want to do with abortion is to permit it but discourage it also." This is the uneasy, ambivalent character of American feelings about abortion, but it can be reflected in public policy, which moves us beyond the current impasse.

What is needed is law that permits abortion but that stipulates both abortion's gravity—homicide—and its antidote in policies that make it less necessary: "It is right that we have the choice, but it would be better if we did not have to make it."

—August 15, 1992

America's death penalty is still an issue

Gov. George W. Bush's comment last February on "Meet the Press" was unequivocal and without qualification: "I am confident that every person who has been put to death in Texas, under my watch, has been guilty of the crime charged, and has had full access to the courts."

Since Bush took office in 1995, no other state has executed even half as many as the 127 put to death in Texas. The governor certainly is in sync with his state, which is adamantly pro-death penalty. Normally I would judge him also to be in step with the majority of U.S. voters and politically astute in linking his presidential qualifications with his capital punishment record. But, after about 15 years of relative dormancy, the death penalty issue may just be boomeranging a bit.

The deluge of pro-execution opinion had all but washed it from mainstream political attention. The issue, however, is re-emerging. The revelation causing this latest discomfort seems to be that miscarriages of justice are not uncommon. In our criminal justice system, mistakes happen.

The concern was great enough to cause Illinois Gov. George Ryan to impose a moratorium on death penalty procedures there until major flaws can be identified and corrected. Religious broadcaster Pat Robertson, a supporter of the death penalty, thinks a moratorium "would indeed be very appropriate." Conservative columnist George Will and the impeccably conservative Cato Institute are expressing serious doubts about the fairness of the death penalty in its present form.

Many who defend capital punishment in principle are troubled by evidence that it's not fairly applied. A number of Texans who believe in capital punishment and support Bush's presidential candidacy are not as sanguine as he about the excellence of the Texas system. In other words, we have a discussion going here. Surprise.

Public opinion apparently has shifted. According to a Gallup poll taken in February, support for the death penalty is the lowest it has been in 19 years (though 66 percent still favor it). The issue of fairness transcends conservative-liberal dichotomies. It is very American to define justice in terms of fairness.

Lest it go unsaid, many religiously motivated persons and groups actively oppose the death penalty. The vast majority of mainline religious communities are on record favoring its abolition, as are the majority of mainline religious ethicists. It is increasingly difficult for an observant Roman Catholic to support capital punishment in good conscience. On the fairness issue, Austin's Bishop John McCarthy has observed that Texas has many examples of indigent defendants served by state-appointed attorneys who "were not prepared to protect the rights of offenders" facing the death penalty.

Bishop McCarthy, of course, opposes the death penalty on more fundamental grounds. Those of us adamantly opposed to it, in season and out of season, know it is neither a demonstrated deterrent to, nor fitting retribution for, murder. Our opposition finally is grounded in religious and moral convictions. We have also recognized all along that it isn't fairly administered and that imperfection in the criminal justice system alone compel its abolition, even if it were otherwise justifiable.

But hey, whatever your reasons. Welcome aboard.

—May 20, 2000

Faith-based ministries are just that

It was 44 years ago this summer that I first visited Koinonia Farm outside of Americus in Sumter County, Ga. The building I was put up in was close to the highway, and bullet holes were in the wall above the bed. In 1956-67, Koinonia was under siege.

Many white people in the neighborhood identified members of Koinonia as non-capitalists and "race-mixers," and therefore it was deemed important to get them out of the county. The persecution in those years was violent, marked by bombings. Shots were fired into the group's houses, at its farm animals—even at its residents. Vandalism, cross burnings, building burnings, Klan Caravans and beatings abounded. I didn't sleep well.

Koinonia Farm is an intentional Christian community founded by Clarence Leonard Jordan (1912-69), a Southern Baptist preacher and visionary. A native of Talbotton, Ga., Jordan was a graduate of the state agricultural college at Athens, where he studied scientific farming in order to help poor farmers have a better life. He then attended the

Southern Baptist Theological Seminary in Louisville, Ky. After six years of study, he received a Ph.D. in Greek New Testament.

He became committed to living or dying by the Sermon on the Mount, by being a loyal participant in what he called the "God Movement," his designation for the biblical Kingdom of God. He was thus both an agrarian and Christian radical. He established Koinonia in 1942 as a demonstration community where Southern people, both white and black, could be taught productive farming while living a communitarian lifestyle based on "the teachings and principles of Jesus."

My next visit to Koinonia was in January 1977, where I talked with Jordan's widow, Florence, and with Millard Fuller, a successful businessman associated with Koinonia. Fuller was telling us about a new organization he and others had just established: Habitat for Humanity. I listened affably, trying to understand the vision, but I must admit the project sounded unrealistic to me. Another one of my insightful judgments.

The organization's success is now a familiar story. Habitat for Humanity International is a nonprofit ecumenical Christian housing ministry "dedicated to eliminating poverty housing and homelessness from the earth." It has constructed more than 100,000 homes, providing at least 500,000 people with simple, decent shelter.

Habitat does its work operating as a voluntary association. Fuller's success is the result of his understanding of New Testament Christianity and his entrepreneurial savvy. His mentor Jordan knew the difference between "the God Movement" and "Caesar."

Jordan, of course, understood that one must render to Caesar the things that are Caesar's. There is an inevitable interfacing with local governments on matters of infrastructure, property acquisition and preparation. Habitat is obliged to cooperate with government in an enterprise that relates to the wider community.

But there is no acceptance of government money for "sticks and bricks"" That is, to build homes. Habitat International is careful that any transactions with HUD do not constitute excessive entanglement with government, which would violate the integrity of its mission.

Religion is a powerful force in American life. It often is a source of impressive services to those in need. To be enthusiastic about the record and role of religion in helping the needy is understandable. President Bush's affirmation of the effectiveness of faith-based social services, therefore, is hard to argue with as a general sentiment. But it's apparent that there are problems with expanding the federal funding of religious groups' services as a matter of public policy.

That's why the president's initiative is facing difficulty as Congress, bureaucrats and religious leaders deal with the details. This is not a matter of technical nit-picking over "Church-State" separation. The point is that religion is not necessarily empowered in its work by direct government involvement. Sometimes it is compromised.

The genius, the strength of voluntary associations is that they are, well, voluntary. Voluntary and uncoerced. Habitat would not be Habitat if it depended on tax money to fund its basic service.

—July 14, 2001

THE STATE

The State

I perhaps have published more articles dealing with "Church-State" relations than on any other topic, many of which were *Religion in America* columns. We are including four columns in our collection: "The Burger Court's legacy on church/state uncertain," "Balancing a secular state within a religious nation," "Justice Brennan: in leadership, in dissent, he makes his church/state mark," and "Dissent in Elkhart and among the Supremes."

The first column was written on the occasion of Chief Justice Warren Burger's retirement from the Supreme Court, over which he presided for seventeen years. He did not turn out to be Richard Nixon's promised "superbly qualified strict constructionist;" he did, however, exert more influence on Establishment-clause jurisprudence than any Supreme Court justice in the twentieth century. It can therefore be argued that Burger has been the most influential justice with regard to the interpretation of the religious Establishment Clause in the Court's entire history! The Burger court's legacy on church-state affairs is more clear to me now than it was in 1986. The Chief Justice was the author of two new guiding jurisprudential concepts: excessive entanglement and accommodation. Both concepts are described in the column.

The second column reflects my conviction that the framers of the constitution intentionally created a secular state in the interests of religious freedom. Church and state were to be separate, a departure from the common wisdom inherited from Europe. This arrangement has been called "our lively experiment." Both James Madison and Thomas

Jefferson were separationists. The word separation is not in the First Amendment, but a separationist philosophy stands behind it and, from 1878-1947, the metaphor of a "wall of separation" was the guiding jurisprudential concept in church-state cases.

I am not an absolute separationist because I think a complete separation of religious groups and the state is impossible. But I am separationist enough to be wary of "excessive entanglement" between them. Rather than the metaphor of a wall of separation, I prefer that of a line of separation. James Madison remarked toward the end of his long public life that he thought we hadn't done such a bad job of drawing the line of separation between church and state. I think the metaphor of the line of separation, a line which is in continual need of revision and extension, serves us well. I try to explain the difference between the nation and the state and that what we have functionally is a secular state in a religious nation. It is not a total separation because the state, at times, participates in civil religious observances. It is important to remember that this nation in which religion thrives has always had a secular tradition along with its religious components.

The third piece on Justice William Brennan's career on the Supreme Court centers on Brennan's position on the relation of the state to religious groups. He was, I argue, "a pragmatic separationist," which describes my own perspective as well as any designation. His vision, I think, was clearer and more consistent than Warren Burger's.

The Elkhart piece is interesting because it is about the Supreme Court's denial of a petition to review a ruling rather than an actual decision. The review was not granted even though Chief Justice William Rehnquist and Justices Antonin Scalia and Clarence Thomas voted to review. The three felt so strongly that they dissented from the denial.

Justice John Paul Stevens then wrote a statement critical of their dissent. All this inter-court conversation over an action without precedental significance! Rehnquist, Scalia, and Thomas are clearly and consistently not separationists. They are accommodationists who do not worry much about government sponsoring or endorsing—"accommodating"—particular religions.

I think this action not to review the appellate court's decision in Elkhart is significant in that it illustrates the fact that the story of religion and government in America has been one of development from state churches to increasing pluralism with a number of temporary "establishments" along the way. The religion clauses have served us well thus far precisely because they provide flexibility of interpretation. It is necessary to look back to original intent, but the Supreme Court, one hopes, also looks around and even forward. The American experience with religion and the state is indeed a lively experiment which requires that we have an eye to evolving precedent and to the needs of the radically pluralistic republic we have become in the twenty-first century.

The Burger Court's legacy on church-state uncertain

The "Burger Court" is history. And among the legacies of Warren E. Burger's 17 years as chief justice of the United States are new interpretations of the religion clauses in the First Amendment.

Some of these new interpretations have had a major impact on public policy, such as decisions affecting governmental financial aid to colleges. Others have been more symbolic—tax-supported nativity scenes in parks, for instance. Still others have dealt with accommodating eccentric religious convictions, such as the refusal to have a photograph taken for a driver's license on religious grounds.

When Burger became chief justice in 1969, the prevailing guiding principle for interpreting the Constitution's religion clauses had been, since 1947, "neutrality." For many years before that, the court had insisted that the First Amendment erected "a wall of separation between Church and State."

In 1970, though, in his first major opinion regarding church-state relations, Burger wrote, "No perfect or absolute separation is really possible; the very existence of the religion clauses is an involvement of sorts—one that seeks to make boundaries to avoid excessive entanglement...We must be also be sure that the end result (of tax exemption for religious groups)—the effect—is not an excessive government entanglement with religion. The test is inescapably one of degree."

Burger clearly believed that "some relationship between government and religious organizations is inevitable." Avoiding "excessive entanglement" became the guiding principle for interpreting the religion clauses.

In a 1971 decision, Burger suggested further tools for deciding the constitutionality of church-state laws: "First, the statute must have a secular legislative purpose; second, its principal or primary effect must be one that neither advances nor inhibits religion....finally, the statute must not foster 'an excessive government entanglement with religion.'"

In the 1980s, Burger took the lead in moving the court to the concept of accomodationism. This perspective, implying an even more positive attitude toward religious groups, holds that nothing in the First Amendment prohibits the state from accommodating those groups in the expression of their faith.

Last year, however, something happened on the way to an accomodationist consensus among the justices. In a 5-4 decision, the court reverted to the concept of neutrality when it struck down an Alabama statute that mandated a moment of silence at the beginning of the public-school day. Writing for the majority, Justice John Paul Stevens stated that such a statute "is not consistent with the established principle that the Government must pursue a course of complete neutrality toward religion."

Burger dissented, claiming that the Alabama law "accommodates the purely private, voluntary religious choices of the individual pupils who wish to pray while at the same time creating a time for non-religious reflection for those who do not choose to pray."

Burger's nominated successor, Justice William Rehnquist, is anything but a strict separationist. Dissenting from the same 1985 opinion, Rehnquist wrote: "The 'wall of separation between church and state' is a metaphor which has proved useless as a guide to judging. It should be frankly and explicitly abandoned." Rehnquist thinks most of the court's opinions on church-state issues since 1947 have reflected "unprincipled decision-making." He will continue to be an articulate proponent of an accomodationist position.

The newly nominated justice, Antonin Scalia, has not published much on church-state matters. Any prediction concerning his philosophy is purely speculative.

Any change in course for the Supreme Court is apt to be neither abrupt nor imminent. Justices Brennan and Marshall must be replaced by persons who agree with President Reagan on matters of religion and the state if there is to be a decisive shift toward a majority accomodationist view. These shifts represent not so much 90-degree turns but more of the cautious negotiation of a track we started on when we began the experiment with religious freedom.

Whatever else Burger may be, he has hardly been a strict constructionist on matters pertaining to the relation between religious groups and the state. Or was he? Have you ever noticed how the designation "strict constructionist" often means "He agrees with my bias"?

—July 12, 1986

Balancing a secular state with a religious nation

The original intent of the framers of the Constitution was to keep the state as separate from religious communities as possible. Yet the Congress that recommended the First Amendment adopted a joint resolution calling for "a day of public Thanksgiving and prayer, to be observed by acknowledging with grateful hearts the many and signal favors of an Almighty God."

President Washington obliged with a proclamation calling on Americans to dedicate such a day "to the services of that great and glorious Being who is the benevolent author of all the good that was, that is, or that will be." And earlier this month, President Reagan called upon the citizens of this great nation "to gather together in homes and places of worship on that day of thanks to affirm by their prayers and their gratitude the many blessings God has bestowed upon us."

The proclamations of Thanksgiving and the principle of separation are not incompatible. There has always been that American tension: We recognize the danger of intermixing church and state, but we also are, as Justice William Douglas once observed, a "religious people whose institutions presuppose a Supreme Being."

It helps to distinguish between "nation" and "state." "Nation," the more comprehensive term, connotes a group of persons bound together by common descent, language or history to form a distinct people. "State," the narrower term, connotes the realm of governance, authority and civil power within such a community. For the past 500 years or so, the nation state has been the world's most common type of political arrangement.

Federalists argued, both before and after the adoption of the Constitution, that America existed as a nation before there was a state. The Union preceded the Constitution. The Constitution was the instrument by which the nation realized an ordered freedom including the freedom of religion.

So Thanksgiving, while authorized by the government, is really an affair of the national community and of individual conscience. Most of us feel that such government involvement in the religious dimension of national life does not constitute excessive entanglement.

According to every poll taken since the late 1930s, almost 19 out of 20 Americans affirm a belief in God. I do not object to spare and tasteful "god" references by public officials on appropriate occasions. Most people who do not believe in "God" believe in some ultimate authority—the Biosphere, the Human Spirit, a Higher Power, or the Common Good. We should perhaps have the understanding that in such pronouncements, "God" means—as Alcoholics Anonymous states in its precepts—whatever you envision "God" to mean. Every major religious tradition values the religious sentiment of gratitude, and even secular humanists are open to reflecting on the fact that life is a gift.

We must recognize, however, that our nation is more radically pluralistic than it was in 1787. The diversities of religious belief are many times greater. In 1943, in a case in which a Jehovah's Witness child was granted relief from having to salute the flag, Justice Robert Jackson wrote: "If there is any fixed star in our constitutional constellation, it is that no official, high or petty, can prescribe what shall be orthodox in politics, nationalism, religion, or other matters of opinion or force citizens to confess by word or act their faith therein." The tension between the secular character of our government and the religious character of our nation is healthy. When kept in proper balance, it ensures religious liberty.

—November 28, 1987

Justice Brennan: In leadership, in dissent, he made his church/state mark

Future appraisals of William J. Brennan's tenure on the Supreme Court may place him among the one or two most effective justices in this century. As tributes to this "beguiling leprechaun" multiply, his contributions to defining the relationship between government and religious groups should be included among those aspects of constitutional interpretation that bear the Brennan mark.

Some justices have been "great dissenters." Others have been able at marshaling consensus and forging majority opinions. Brennan did both remarkably well. In church-state matters, he did so as a "pragmatic separationist." At one extreme, strict separationists say there should be a wall between the two realms. Leo Pfeffer of the American Jewish Congress advocates an absolute separation, which he concedes is unattainable, "else what's a secularist heaven for?"

At the other extreme, accommodationists believe the Constitution not only does *not* require complete separation but *does* require that government accommodate religion.

Former Chief Justice Warren Burger wrote that the Constitution "affirmatively mandates accommodation" of all religions because anything less would require "callous indifference."

Justice Brennan was not as strict as Pfeffer, but certainly not as accommodating as Chief Justice William Rehnquist or Justices Byron White, Sandra Day O'Connor, Antonin Scalia and Anthony Kennedy. Separationists are despondent, and accomodationists are smiling in the wake of his retirement.

He was a wily politician who often recruited support by anticipating his colleagues' concerns and then incorporating them in majority opinions characterized by lucidity and common sense. His dissents often were longer and more scholarly than the majority opinion.

One unlikely majority opinion he put together was in a 1985 case involving a contract under which a public school district in Grand Rapids, Mich., leased space in a parochial school. Brennan led the Court in finding the shared-time program unconstitutional: "The Community Education and Shared Time programs have the 'primary or principal effect' of advancing religion."

While noting the important role non-public schools have played in American education and recognizing the right of parents to choose between public and private, Brennan wrote that the Establishment Clause "rests on the belief that a union of government and religion tends to destroy government and to degrade religion."

My favorite Brennan dissent occurred in a 1984 case in which the Court decided that a nativity scene sponsored by the city of Pawtucket, R.I., was constitutional. In what I consider a foolish and mischievous argument, Chief Justice Burger reasoned that the creche along with Santa Claus, reindeer, candy-striped poles, Christmas trees and a teddy bear was evidence of secular intent.

Brennan dissented: "I refuse to accept the notion implicit in today's decision that non-Christians would find that the religious content of the creche is eliminated by the fact that it appears as part of the city's otherwise secular celebration of the Christmas holiday...

"It is the chief symbol of the characteristically Christian belief that a divine Savior was brought into the world and that the purpose of this miraculous birth was to illuminate a path toward salvation and redemption. For Christians, that path is exclusive, precious, and holy.

"But for those who do not share these beliefs, the symbolic reenactment of the birth of a divine being who has been miraculously incarnated as a man stands as a dramatic reminder of their differences with the Christian faith."

An Irish-Catholic from New Jersey, Brennan had a vision of constitutional construction that wasn't strict enough for today's court. But alas, I confess that I will miss the man who conceded: "I read the Constitution in the only way that I can: as a Twentieth-Century American. I look to the history of the time of framing and to the intervening history of interpretation, of course. But the ultimate question must be, what do the words of the text mean in our time? For the genius of the Constitution rests not in any static meaning it might have had in a world that is dead and gone, but in the adaptability of its great principles to cope with current problems and current needs."

That can't be totally wrong-headed, can it?

—August 11, 1990

Dissent in Elkhart and among the Supremes

An occurrence in the U.S. Supreme Court this week was interesting. The court denied a petition for a review of a ruling that a 6-foot-high granite monument inscribed with the Ten Commandments, which stands in front of the Municipal Building in Elkhart, Ind., is an unconstitutional establishment of religion.

Four votes are required for a review to be granted. Three justices—Chief Justice Rehnquist, with Justices Scalia and Thomas—dissented from the denial. Justice Stevens then wrote a statement critical of their dissent. This jockeying around without precedential significance reflects deep fissures in American society as well as in the court.

The largest portion of the monument in dispute contains the text of the Commandments. At the top are two small tablets that contain biblical Hebrew script. Surrounding them is a floral design, and between them is an all-seeing eye within a pyramid. Immediately below the eye is an eagle clutching an American flag. Below the text are two small Stars of David. In the center of the two stars is a Chi-Rho symbol representing Christ.

The U.S. Court of Appeals for the Seventh Circuit in Chicago held that the monument fails to pass what is known as the three-part Lemon test for church-state legislation:

- The statute must have a secular purpose.
- Its primary effect must be neither to advance nor to prohibit religion.
- It must not foster excessive entanglement between church and state.

The Seventh Circuit Court found that the display violates the first and second prongs of the test, noting that Supreme Court precedents "simply prevent government at any level from intruding into the religious life of our people by sponsoring or endorsing a particular perspective on religious matters."

The three dissenting justices not only disagree with denying review but discuss the merits of the case, arguing that the monument's presence is not unconstitutional. None of the three is a proponent of the Lemon test in the first place, but they all conclude that its standards, at any rate, are not violated.

Justice Stevens in his "statement" points out that the dissent "omits one extremely significant fact and discounts another." He notes that the first two lines of the monument's text appear in significantly larger type than the remainder: "The Ten Commandments—I AM the LORD they GOD." The two Stars of David and the Chi-Rho, Stevens argues, "are hard to square with the proposition that the monument expresses no particular religious preference."

The discounted fact is that at the dedication ceremony in 1958 the three principal speakers were a Catholic priest, a Protestant minister, and a Jewish rabbi. None of the three spoke of the "cross cultural significance" of the Ten Commandments.

In reading background material regarding the Elkhart monument case, including the major points in each religious leader" remarks, I think that the original intent was not secular cross-cultural-Western-legal tradition in character, but rather a religious interfaith statement.

It was one part a "Protestant-Catholic-Jew" vision, to use a phrase made popular by the late Will Herberg's 1955 book by that title. It was another part American Civil Religion, as expressed by Rabbi M.E. Finkelstein of Elkhart's

Temple Israel, who thought that the event "should be an occasion for the dedication of everyone to the high ideals inherent in the American way of life."

It worked in Elkhart in 1958. But it is inadequate for Elkhart and the rest of the nation today. Multiculturalism in 2001 requires a wider vision, encompassing a more diverse and crowded public square. The adjustments often are accompanied by pain. The high court is not the only divided institution in our land.

—June 2, 2001

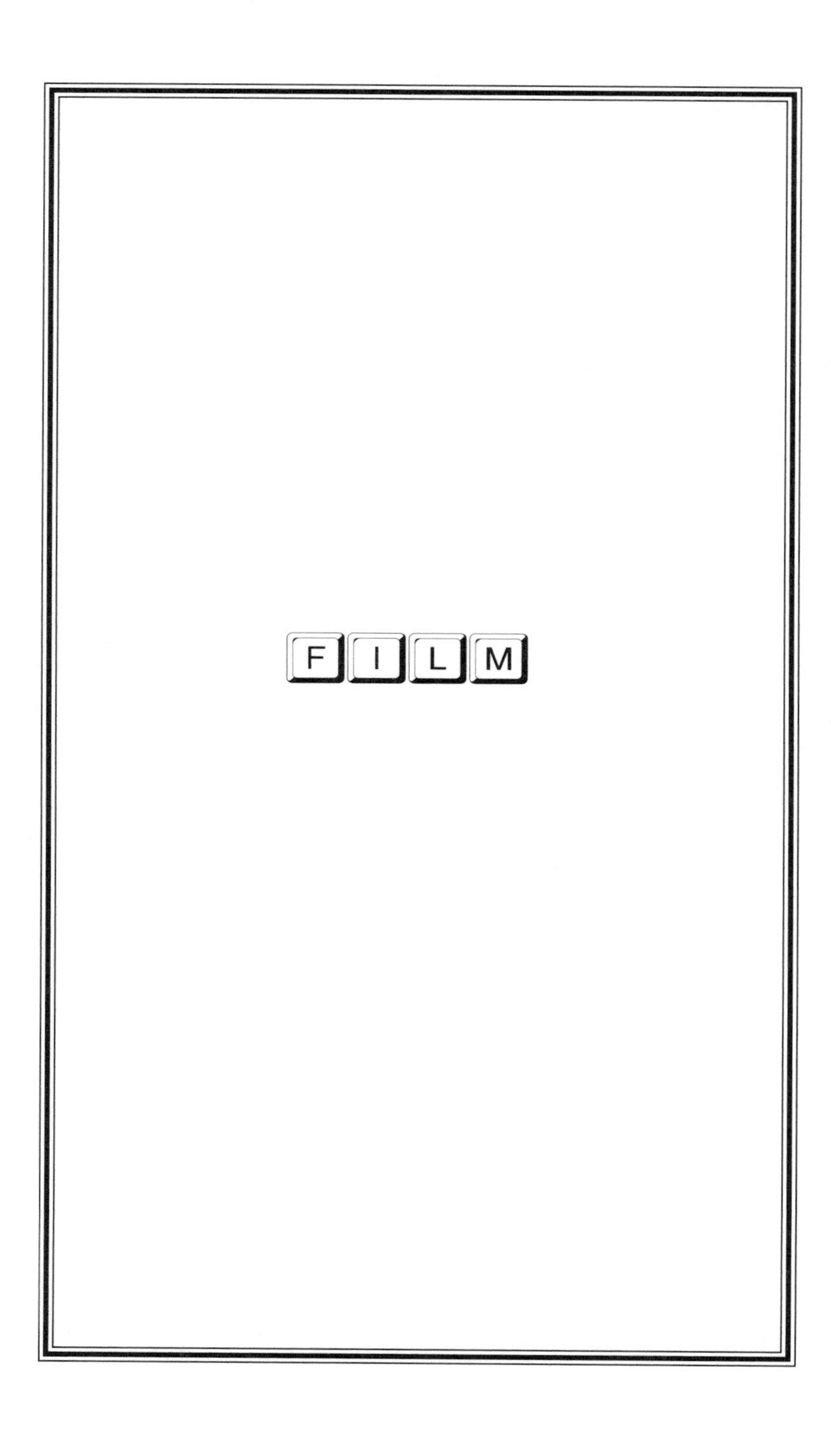
F I L M

Film

As difficult as any part of the selection process was deciding what not to include in motion picture criticism. I think I lapsed into thinking too highly of my work as film critic. I was a bit too proud of my ruminations on Stanley Kubrick's "Eyes Wide Shut," or Spike Lee's "Summer of Sam." The reality is that my recognition as film critic has yet to take hold. The four choices, spanning fourteen column years, constitute what is probably a modest and realistic sampling of this less than overwhelming component of my writing.

Martin Scorsese's film, "The Last Temptation of Christ." was quite controversial. The fact that I had to see it in Evanston, Ill. is a reminder that cities such as Tallahassee, Fl. didn't show it. I wrote about it before viewing it advocating artistic freedom and tolerance. After seeing the film I had a feeling similar to the one I had after reading Kazantzakis's novel in the late 1960s: interesting, but not compelling. "'Temptation' is flawed but serious and should be seen" was a headline which sums up my recommendation. What I said in my criticism is, in retrospect, rather standard stuff, but I hope not totally boilerplate.

Director Robert Zemeckis's film, "Contact," was the occasion for the column "On science, religion and Jodie Foster." It is included primarily because it drew significant comment at the time.

"'Star Wars': the phantom faith menace" may be closer to boilerplate. The main reason for choosing this column is that the Star Wars creations have been a major force in American popular culture for well over two decades. I am not certain that "Episode I—The Phantom Menace" actually succeeds as part of a prequel to the original trilogy, but it succeeds to a reasonable degree in updating a saga which has fired the imagination of millions of Americans. It is difficult for one who is interested in religion and popular culture to avoid dealing with the Star Wars phenomenon.

"'O Brother, Where Art Thou?' should not be overlooked" was a column motivated by precisely what the title states. I thought that this film was left behind in the promotion of more blockbuster productions. The column apparently gave a modest boost to local attendance of "O Brother." The classical and biblical themes played out in 1930's deep South settings work. There are some captivating scenes which kind of take the viewer by surprise. The historical antecedents of this version of the film are themselves interesting. I wrote a later column on a documentary of the music in "O Brother," titled "Down from the Mountain." I commented in the second column that "the piety is Protestant Christian specific, but it transcends its particular situation of origin to evoke themes and feelings that are accessible to most all of us." I think this is true of both the film and the documentary.

'Temptation' is flawed but serious and should be seen

I finally saw *The Last Temptation of Christ* in the old Chicago suburb of Evanston, Ill., the home of impressive church buildings, Northwestern University and the Women's Christian Temperance Union. It proved worth the trouble to squeeze the viewing into my visit to Evanston for academic business.

"Last Temptation" is vintage Martin Scorsese: direct, impatient and intimate, the camera quickly penetrating to what he feels is the heart of the matter. The film captures

Nikos Kazantzakis's vision of human life as a struggle between flesh and spirit. As Jesus, Willem Dafoe ("Platoon") successfully portrays the tormented pilgrimage from frustrated and confused carpenter to strong and confident Christ.

Barbara Hershey as Mary Magdalene is convincing as a woman whose prostitution is a form of protest, the result of earlier rejection and disillusion. Her activities in the brothel are not portrayals of erotic celebration but rather the weary work of a strong woman whose true character belies her fallen state.

The special relationship between Jesus and Judas (Harvey Keitel) is typical of the emphasis of author Kazantzakis and director Scorsese on male bonding, a kind of buddy-system approach to life's struggles. Jesus persuades Judas, whose discernment is light-years ahead of the other disciples, to betray him in order to fulfill God's plan.

The film is saturated with blood and violence, sex and eccentric interpretation. The Bible, of course, is also filled with sex and violence, and the New Testament focuses on a bloody crucifixion as the price of salvation. The film does not celebrate mindless violence, and the sexual scenes are tasteful and integral to the story. It is neither pornographic nor obscene.

The film is interesting and provocative, but ultimately it fails. Scorsese interjects into a starkly realistic interpretation a rather bothersome symbolism. In the desert the temptations come to Jesus in the form of a serpent, a lion and an archangel (Satan) in the form of a flame. Blood pours out of an apple Jesus eats. In one scene Jesus reaches into his body and pulls out his heart for the disciples to admire. A rather crude allusion, one gathers, to Roman Catholic devotion to the Sacred Heart of Jesus. There is also an apparent portrayal of the eucharistic doctrine of transubstantiation when, at the Last Supper, the wine turns to blood. It doesn't work...for me.

The more basic quarrel I have with "Temptation" is theological. Scorsese follows Kazantzakis closely, and the film therefore inherits the novel's congenital failure. The biblical story of Christ is not a spiritual quest narrative. Kazantzakis portrays Christ as the Nietzschean hero who wrests divinity from the struggle of flesh with spirit: Zorba the Messiah. Sort of "Local prophet makes good," or "Nazareth boy achieves Godhead." Kazantzakis and his followers are romantics and the Christian Gospel is not romantic literature.

I think "Temptation" is inferior to "Taxi Driver," "The Color of Money" and "Raging Bull," other Scorsese films that have dealt with religious dimensions. But one of the virtues of the film, and the novel on which it is based, is that they shock us into recognizing the essential strangeness of the Gospel narrative. The story can become so domesticated in liturgy and catechetical instruction that it grows stale. Kazantzakis revives our sense of the dimension of madness in the original message.

Many adult Christians (and others) will benefit from seeing "Last Temptation." It is a serious work of art, and to prevent its playing is both intolerant and un-Christian. Many studies have established that religious commitment does not correlate well with tolerance and openness. It should.

The film is not blasphemous, because Scorsese (Roman Catholic heretic that he may be) and screenwriter Paul Schrader (an observant Christian) did not intend to defame Jesus. "Temptation" is not—as Joseph Reilly, director of Morality in Media, claims—"an intentional attack on Christianity."

As I left the Evanston Theatre, three persons were handing out New Testaments—at 11 p.m. They were members of Evanston's First Presbyterian Church. Each had seen the film. One liked it, one had mixed feelings and one disliked it. They invited people to compare "Temptation" with the Gospel narratives and invited us to a forum the congregation was sponsoring as a Christian Education project. What an imaginative and effective way to engage the film! Because they had seen the film, their witness had credibility. Their approach was more appropriate than lockstep opposition and uninformed sloganeering. If I were teaching an adult church-school class, I would suggest we see the film and then compare it with the biblical record and Christian theological interpretation.

Numerous petitions protesting the film have circulated in Tallahassee. It is a pity that in Tallahassee, the state's capital, home of many impressive religious congregations and two major universities, theater owners are intimidated to the point that they fail to allow freedom of serious artistic expression and religious discussion.

—September 17, 1988

On science, religion, and Jodie Foster

Last week I received a call from a *Charlotte Observer* reporter asking me whether I had seen the movie "Contact." I had been referred to him for a story he was writing on the relation between science and religion. He also had heard about a course on evolution that I will be team-teaching in the fall and was wondering if it would focus on the conflict between science and religion. At the time of our conversation, I was running behind on my summer cinema schedule.

I have since seen "Contact," based on the late Carl Sagan's novel and directed by Robert Zemeckis. Jodie Foster stars as Ellie Arroway, an astronomer obsessed with the search for extraterrestrial intelligence. Matthew McConaughey plays Palmer Joss, a prophet-theologian equally obsessed with the search for meaning. Other characters, rather stereotypical, are David Drumlin, a cynical establishment scientist; S.R. Hadden, a character who is half Howard Hughes, half Daddy Warbucks; and Richard Rank, a thinly veiled version of Christian Right leader Ralph Reed.

"Contact" is not just another sensationalist sci-fi movie, in part because of its treatment of the relation between religion and science. It captures something of the complexity of the subject. Foster plays a scientist who is ostensibly an agnostic, but who ironically displays the awe, humility, idealism, hope and vision that are typically viewed as religious virtues. They are contrasted with the vices displayed by more conventionally religious folk in the film—defensiveness, exclusivism, and hostility.

Although Ellie can never bring herself to say the "F" word—faith—she is indeed a person of faith. Faith, at least in the biblical sense of the word, is personal trust and loyalty to a cause. She is a virtual Joan of Arc—a Knight of Faith—in search of answers to who we are and why we are here.

As I suggested to the Charlotte journalist, science and religion have not always been in a state of war. To be sure, there has been much conflict, from Galileo in the seventeenth-century to the proponents of Creation Science who oppose Darwinian theory. But there have also been religious thinkers who have made science the keystone of their faith. Rather than religion *against* science, a religion *of* science, so to speak. Robert G. Ingersoll, the nineteenth–century American religious humanist, made Darwin his Moses.

The late Roman Catholic theologian Pierre Teilhard de Chardin synthesized evolutionary science and religion. For Chardin, religion completes evolution. Still other religious thinkers have suggested that science and religion deal with two different realms: description and meaning. Mc-

Conaughey's character, Palmer Joss, takes this position in the film. Science describes the way the cosmos is or seems to be. But science cannot impute value or meaning to the way humans experience the cosmos.

I'll leave criticism of "Contact" as an expression of the sci-fi literary and cinematic genre to those more qualified to judge. As an exploration of the relationship between science and religion, however, "Contact' is well ahead of the curve for popular treatments of the topic.

—July 26, 1997

"Star Wars:" the phantom faith menace

Dare to say no to Star Wars? Good luck. The series has become so embedded in our popular culture that trying to avoid it is to resist a powerful force (not to be confused with the Force).

Ignoring it also is uncool. "Star Wars: Episode I—The Phantom Menace" is the first of three episodes in a prequel to the original trilogy built around the struggle between Luke Skywalker and Darth Vader. "Phantom Menace" has not lived up to its hype, but it fulfills realistic expectations. There are breathtaking backdrops, state-of-the-art special effects, new places and new faces. The computer-generated bestiary is imaginative. It's fun.

A number of critics have been tough on the "The Phantom Menace." David Steritt, writer for *The Christian Science Monitor*, suggests it's a great adventure for the eye, but that we "find little heart and no real soul." Others join him in a collective lament that George Lucas, the series creator, is more interested in aliens than he is in humans. Dazzling effects, but no real character development.

Such reviews probably are to be expected given the promotional campaign that practically guaranteed disappointment and to our 22 years of familiarity with Star War creations. Other reviewers such as Roger Ebert of *The Chicago Sun Times* judge it to be "an astonishing achievement in imaginative film making." Lively debate regarding the series continues and one of the ongoing discussions has to do with religious motifs.

Bill Moyers's interview with Lucas in *Time* (April 25), has contributed to popular discussion of "the true theology of Star Wars." Lucas states that he consciously dealt with classical religious themes. He drew from Christian, Hindu and other religious traditions as well as from the monsters of Greek mythology. I think I also detected Buddhist and Taoist motifs.

Apparently Lucas also has drawn from the work of the late Joseph Campbell, one of the most influential interpreters of myth in our time. Campbell's 1949 book, "*The Hero With a Thousand Faces*" suggests some of the hero themes in the Star Wars epic.

There also have been less than positive responses to the saga from some religious communities. Its eclectic character offends some orthodox believers. Others feel its theology is blatantly heretical. But it is as difficult for religious groups to avoid Star Wars as it is for the general public. Probably the more useful response is to engage the stories critically, comparing them with the teachings of one's own faith tradition. Many young adults who grew up on Star Wars find such discussions quite interesting.

Faith and fantasy can mix. The late C.S. Lewis, Oxford literary scholar, used science fiction to present sophisticated interpretations of Christian tenets. He wrote outerplanetary fantasies that had deep religious and moral overtones. Lewis's "Chronicles of Narnia," for instance, was a series of allegorical fantasies.

Icons of good and evil; the fall from grace and redemption; the need for all organisms to live for mutual advantage; all of these themes are transparently presented in the series. The dark side of the Force does have to be faced and resisted. Right.

Now, what does that mean? What is the meaning of heroes? Is Lucas correct in his assumption that the issues we face today "are the same ones that existed 3,000 years ago?" These are great questions. Knock Star Wars or become something of a devotee. Avoiding it is difficult.

—June 5, 1999

'O Brother, Where Art Thou?' should not be overlooked

A bit of a sleeper overshadowed by blockbuster films this season is one that engages religion and culture in an interesting way. "O Brother, Where Art Thou?" is directed by the brothers Coen, Joel and Ethan, of "Fargo" fame. The religion is primarily evangelical Protestant, the culture Depression-era Mississippi.

The film is based on Homer's "Odyssey" to an extent that belabors the obvious. George Clooney's leading character is named Ulysses Everett McGill. Ulysses and his two companions, Pete and Delmar, escape from a southern prison farm and begin a peculiar odyssey.

Their first personal encounter is with a black prophet-poet who is, of course, blind. They are seduced by three sirens operating from a Mississippi river bank. There is the requisite cyclopean figure, "Big Dan," a hustler-salesman with an eye patch.

Interesting to film buffs is that other sources for the screenplay are the movies directed by Preston Sturges during World War II. James M. Wall, *Christian Century* journalist and film critic, argues that the Coens took their title and much of their plot for "where Art Thou" from a 1941 Sturges film titled "Sullivan's Travels." They apparently also based the characters of a politician (Gov. Pappy O'Daniel) and his doltish son on another Sturges film, "Hail the Conquering Hero" (1944).

Of interest to the general moviegoer is the way in which religious themes are dealt with in the episodic adventures of Ulysses, Pete and Delmar. Included are conversion; forgiveness; retribution; piety and popular culture; and religious-based ideology. The whole nine yards!

Ulysses, articulate to the point of rhetorical overkill, often serves as a secular foil to his more religious companions beliefs, dismissing their "miracles" with "perfectly scientific explanations" for their close escapes. Two scenes are memorable. The first is an outdoor baptismal service with a choir processing to the riverbank singing "Down to the River to Pray." Pete and Delmar get baptized. Ulysses remains self-consciously the objective observer. The second is a massive Ku Klux Klan night meeting. Its choreography is arresting. The rhetoric accurately reflects the religious component of Klan thinking. The event reminds one of the relative legitimacy of the Klan in the 1920s and '30s and of its pathetic illegitimacy in retrospect.

"Where Art Thou" stays just this side of parody. It employs stereotype in a measured and intentional manner that works. It is classical in content as well as form. A brutal and ineffective prison system; politicians who verge on the demagogic as they grope for a strategy that fits what they perceive people want to hear; the role of popular music, religious and secular, in assuaging the pain and alienation of the working poor; the enduring millennialism of a Ulysses McGill who envisions a transformed South, characterized as a “veritable age of reason.” These are subjects that are hardly anachronistic in 2001.

The film is properly classified as comedy. But because of the vanities and illusions of the characters and of the society in which they are situated, its comedy passes over into irony. There are many ironic elements in American history in general, and in the Southern experience in particular. The biblical squint on the human situation is more ironic than tragic or pathetic.

So…if you want trenchant social criticism and insight into the solution of the national drug problem, see “Traffic.” If you want imaginative escape and restorative fantasy, see “Crouching Tiger, Hidden Dragon.” But if you’re interested in something of a postmodern reinterpretation of Southern religion and culture in the early 1940s, see “O Brother, Where Art Thou.”

—April 7, 2001

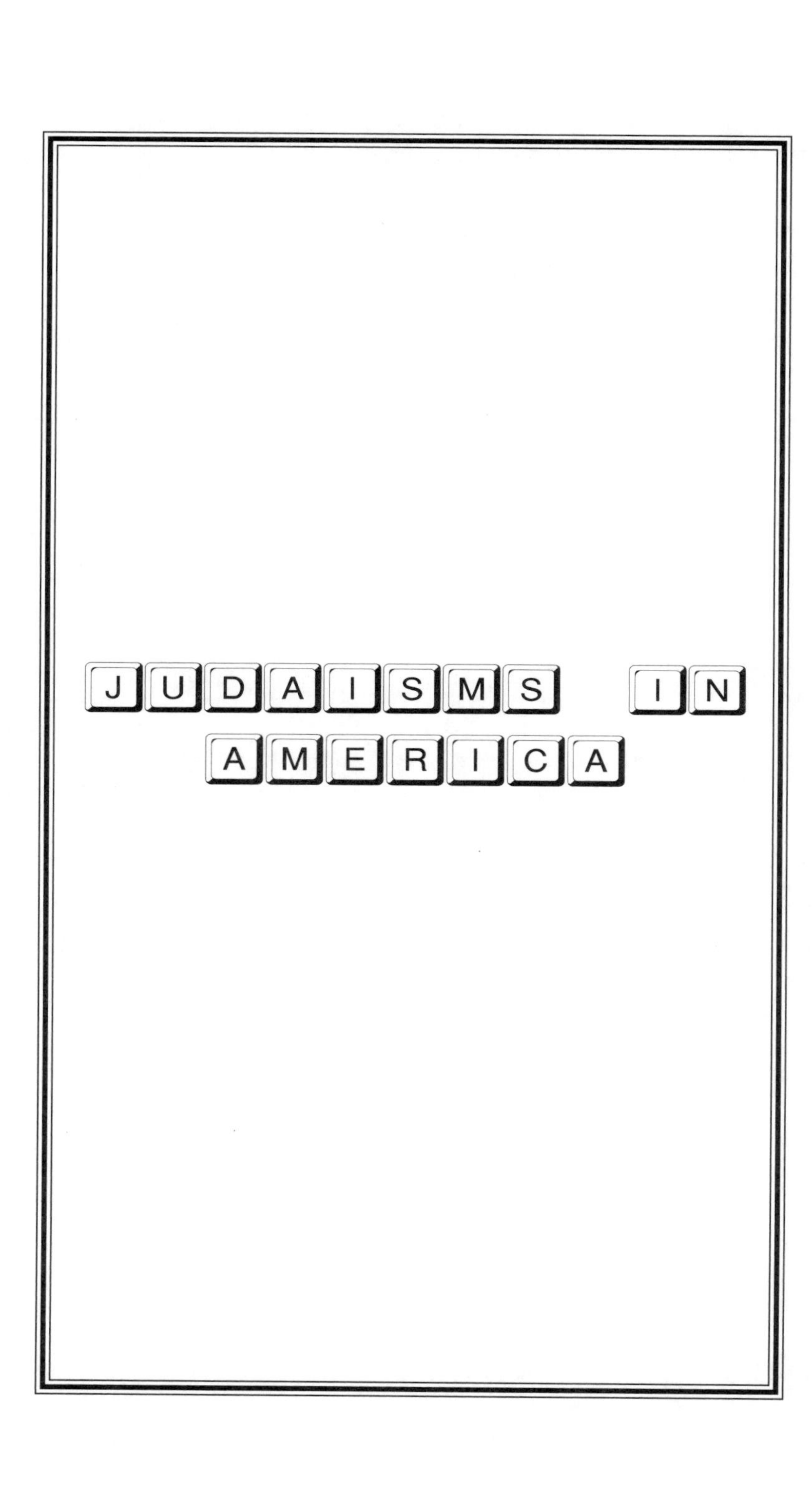
JUDAISMS IN
AMERICA

Judaisms in America

One of the abiding joys through the years has been my friendship with many members of the Jewish community, particularly with Rabbi Stanley and Vivian Garfein and members of Temple Israel, the only synagogue in Tallahassee when we arrived in 1969. I am less familiar with, but impressed by the quality of community life at the Shomrei Torah Congregation, the Conservative Synagogue established twenty years into our residency. Earlier studies and experiences in Boston contributed to an appreciation for things Jewish. I developed a love for the Hebrew Bible and almost took doctoral training in what was called "Old Testament" where I was then studying. My first teaching role when I was a graduate student at Boston University was as a lecturer in Hebrew Bible. There were several rabbis in the Boston Area who were eloquent champions of social justice during the 1950s and 1960s. And during the civil rights movement I became an admirer of Abraham Joshua Heschel, perhaps the most influential theologian in American Jewish history.

"American Jews remember what their parents forgot," was among my earliest *Religion in America* columns. It basically is a broadstroke review of the religious Jewish experience in the United States. A number of columns followed on such specific subjects as American Jews and Israel, Jews in American politics, and Jews and the religious right. But this selection is appropriate in that it was the introductory entry for many subsequent columns.

"Three cheers for tolerance on Rosh Hashana" was a direct response to a an op-ed piece by Dennis Prager arguing that American Jews should be more accepting of "public expressions" of Christianity in order to keep anti-Semitism at bay. I think Prager's analysis and argument are wrong. I am told that this column, or excerpts from it were read in the Rosh Hashana service by the president of Temple Israel the week of its publication.

"U.S. Judaism is diverse yet thriving" is the last of a type of column that has become *de rigueur* around the high holy days when the pulse of American Judaism is taken and pronouncements regarding its health soberly offered. I offered my share of "how is Judaism doing?" columns through the years. It did—does—seem to me that 2000 was an extraordinary year for Jewish visibility in the United States. It was not just, or even primarily, Joseph Lieberman's candidacy, but a number of signs of Jewish excellence shot through and through American culture, to which the senator's vice-presidential nomination was symbolic confirmation.

American Jews remember what their parents forgot

A while back I was host to a visiting professor from a distinguished American law school. The professor, a native of New York City, mentioned that he had been raised in a Jewish home where religious customs were not observed. But his own family now attends a conservative synagogue and tries to keep dietary laws, and his two children attend Hebrew school. His father is both surprised and somewhat perplexed that the professor's family was religiously observant.

This is an example of "Hansen's Law," formulated by historian Marcus Hansen: "What the son wishes to forget, the grandson remembers." Hansen studied the phenomenon of the third-generation immigrant. He demonstrated that these people, no longer "foreign" or struggling to survive, sustain their Americanness but also confirm their ties to their forebears—for the sake of a heritage they now want to remember.

American Jews join with members of their faith around the world this week to celebrate the High Holy Days. At sundown last Sunday, Jews ushered in the new year 5746; on Wednesday, the 10 days of introspection will end with Yom Kippur, the Day of Atonement.

American Judaism in 1985 is the creation of the third generation's effort to remember what its parents forgot. Professor Jacob Neusner, a prominent academic authority on Judaism, has observed that this is the first generation in centuries to be able to decide in an open society whether to be Jewish.

Many people have worried over the survival of Judaism in a free America. The enduring problem for Jews in this country is the threat of total assimilation into American society. What Hitler failed to accomplish, American pluralism and secularity might yet accomplish. Rabbi Arthur Hertzberg and other writers have suggested that American Jewry is an endangered species.

Of course, a degree of assimilation has been necessary for the survival of the Jewish community in all ages. What many identify as Jewish cuisine, for instance, was originally simply Eastern European food. Spanish Jewry used Greek philosophy in its expression of Judaism. Palestinian Jewry used Roman methods of legal codification.

Reform Judaism, the dominant Jewish movement in nineteenth-century America, went far toward accommodating Judaism to American culture. Orthodoxy, the branch of Judaism for most of the 3.5 million Jews who came from Russia, Poland, Romania, Hungary, and Austria between 1890 and 1920, opposed accommodation with "gentile culture." Conservative Judaism took shape as the middle ground. One ironic factor that has threatened Jewish survival in America is the relative lack of anti-Semitism.

In the past anti-Semitism has contributed to a sense of Jewish identity and community cohesion. In America it crested during the half-century preceding World War II. Since then, surveys have reflected diminishing levels of Jew hatred. As journalist/scholar Charles E. Silberman points out: "There is no longer enough anti-Semitism in America to hold the community together."

Jonathan D. Sarna, an expert in American Jewish history, concludes that if the experience in America has not been utter heaven for Jews, "it has been as far from Hell as Jews in the Diaspora have ever known."

In a new and remarkably upbeat book, A *Certain People: American Jews and Their Lives Today*, Silberman notes that Jews are integrated into American society to a degree undreamed of a generation ago. Virtually every occupation is now open to them. Positions from chairman and chief executive officer of the DuPont Corporation to secretary of state are now attainable.

Silberman also argues that, contrary to a common anxiety concerning the extinction of American Judaism, there is also a Jewish cultural and religious renaissance under way. The consensus seems to be that Jews in America have never had it so good. Will the current comfortable position be short-lived? Not if Jews, like others in our pluralistic culture, choose to affirm their religious and ethnic heritage.

As the law professor realized, to be or not to be observant is an option, not a requirement, in a free and open society.

—September 21, 1985

Three cheers for tolerance on Rosh Hashana

Beware of the shibboleths of "tolerance" and "diversity." That is the advice recently given to the U.S. Jewish community by Dennis Prager, talk-show host and a director of Empower America. In a *Wall Street Journal* op-ed piece, Prager maintains that the more American Jews oppose any public expression of Christianity, the more they weaken their own community and increase their vulnerability to anti-Semitism.

Prager's argument is interesting and probably wrong enough to cause serious mischief. He holds that the American Jewish establishment inadvertently undermines the nation's Judeo-Christian foundation by not realizing that American Christians "are not the Christians of Europe past." Sectarian Protestantism, through a unique form of religious tolerance (this tolerance apparently was not a "shibboleth"), established a moral foundation that is the glue that keeps our diverse civilization from cracking. The problem, according to Prager, is that too many American Jews, because of Europe's history of anti-Semitism, "instinctively oppose any public expression of Christianity." He reminds his fellow Jews that "America remains the most tolerant (not that "shibboleth" again), open and Judaism-loving country Jews have ever lived in." In this country, he concludes, the seeds of anti-Semitism are planted by the rejection of Christianity.

There is less to Prager's argument and advice than meets the eye. I am aware of no reflexive Jewish opposition to public expressions of Christianity unless the "public" means state-sponsored expressions. Where is there organized or unorganized Jewish opposition to Christians doing their thing so long as they do it in the voluntary sector? But not in tax-supported institutions with implied official sponsorship. The Anti-Defamation League objects to such expressions. So do I.

There has been less incidence of anti-Semitism in the United States than in European nations for a number of reasons. Our republic was invented as the first post-Enlightenment Western nation, and we had no centuries-old tradition of anti-Semitism. Then, too, we have always practiced diversity in our bigotry. There is no single scapegoat group.

Perhaps the greatest reason for the relatively low degree of anti-Semitism has been the effective work of the ADL in monitoring and exposing it whenever and wherever it appears. Vigilance is the price of tolerance for religious minorities.

Tallahassee provides a case history in tolerance and diversity illustrating my point. When I came here in 1969, I spent a significant amount of time, as an invited non-Jew, attending meetings of committees hastily formed to protest some form of Christian-majority activity that was insensitive, not to say unconstitutional: Gideons passing out New Testaments accompanied by prayers and invitations to Christian discipleship to third-graders during school hours, for instance. There is much less of this in Tallahassee than there was 30 years ago. But not because the Jewish community lay low out of fear of anti-Semitic backlash.

Prager's notion of a Judeo-Christian America was classically expressed by the late Will Herberg in his 1955 book, *Protestant-Catholic-Jew.* Today it is Protestant, Catholic, Jew, and many others too. On this Rosh Hashana, may observant Jews enter 5760 remembering that there is no religious establishment in this country. Not even a "Judeo-Christian" religious establishment.

—September 11, 1999

U.S. Judaism is diverse yet thriving

On Rosh Hashana, pundits who focus on religion and culture predictably take the pulse of U.S. Judaism to see how it fares. Sort of an annual physical. And spiritual.

Some will speak the language of crisis—"The Vanishing American Jew"—while others will report post-crisis signs of renewed vigor. I have learned that there usually is compelling evidence to support either view.

Recent Jewish visibility on the national public square has been both high and positive. Al Gore's selection of U.S. Sen. Joseph Lieberman as his vice-presidential running mate, in addition to resuscitating the Democratic presidential campaign, has provided the occasion for all kinds of instruction regarding the different branches of Judaism. In a time when Federal Reserve Board Chairman Alan Greenspan, former Treasury Secretary Robert Rubin and Supreme Court Justices Ruth Bader Ginsberg and Stephen Breyer have such an impact on our lives, Lieberman's selection is more symbolic confirmation than substantial breakthrough.

Another milestone worth noting is the Jewish statement on Christians and Christianity published Sept. 10. "Dabru Emet," taken from the biblical phrase "speak the truth to one another," was signed by more than 150 rabbis and scholars from all branches of Judaism. The document notes that recent years have seen "a dramatic and unprecedented shift in Jewish and Christian relations." It then affirms, "We believe these changes merit a thoughtful Jewish response...We believe it is time for Jews to learn about the efforts of Christians to honor Judaism."

This document is significant in that it was written and signed by Jewish thinkers who differ on important issues and because it admonishes Jews to get up to speed regarding newer Christian understandings of Christianity's peculiar relationship with Judaism: Dabru Emet wrestles with both Jewish and interfaith diversity.

The important book of the year dealing with Jews in the United States is Samuel Freedman's *Jew vs. Jew: The Struggle for the Soul of American Jewry*. It's interesting, informative and provocative. Freedman, a veteran journalist and now journalism professor, examines seven case histories that demonstrate the diversity, even strife, among and within the various branches of Judaism. Juda*isms* in America, he reminds us, is more to the point than Juda*ism* in America.

It is an oft-noted paradox that North American traditions of religious freedom have provided for unprecedented Jewish acceptance and success while North American cultural diversity has provided the occasion for both internal division and even decline. Two observations:

- I do not, finally, interpret the American Jewish situation as all that exceptional. Shaped by our pluralist character and our tradition of religious freedom, we legitimated on a national scale what literary critic Mary Louise Pratt has called a contact zone: "the space in which peoples geographically and historically separated come into contact with each other and establish ongoing relations." It is not just Jews who have to deal creatively with the tension between tradition and cultural diversity, between serious commitment and genuine openness to others. Many of us are called to share this tension.
- I am more impressed with symptoms of revival than decline. Intermarriage and assimilation are not news; more intense religious fervor and ferment in the Judaisms are.

So from those of us who are not members of the tribe, happy New Year! And, speaking as a Gentile, best wishes for your continued success in managing America's splendid pluralist tension.

—September 30, 2000

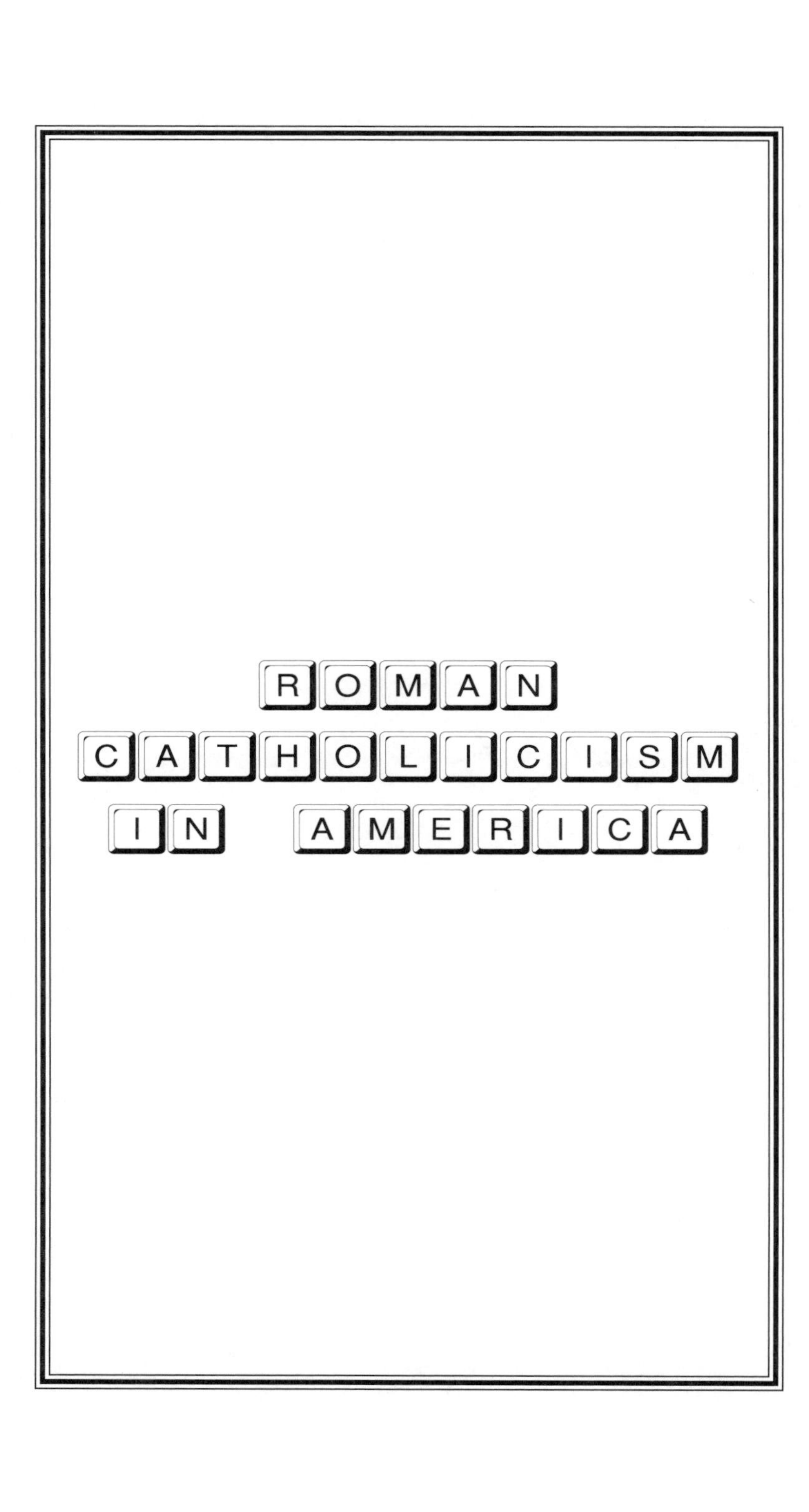
ROMAN
CATHOLICISM
IN AMERICA

Roman Catholicism in America

As was the case with Judaism, I wrote many columns on various aspects of Roman Catholicism in the United States. Often representatives of the Catholic Church or lay communicants would publicly or privately thank me when they agreed with my comments. When my columns were critical of some aspect of Church policy, there would be the predictable follow up letter to the editor from my friend and frequent ally who was with the Florida Catholic Conference admonishing me to remember that the "Catholic Church is not a democracy" and that there is more to the Church than my post-Vatican Council II understanding can comprehend. He advised that I need to listen more to the bishops, less to Catholic theologians.

"Catholic bishops' economic ideas don't match traditional American views of wealth" was my commentary on the U.S. Conference of Catholic Bishops pastoral letter of 1986. In that decade the bishops issued two prophetic pastorals, this one and an earlier one (1983) on nuclear weapons. The gist of my column is that the traditional Roman Catholic bias toward the alleviation of poverty through policies of distributive justice are in tension with received American notions concerning poverty. Accompanying my column that day was a book review about Dorothy Day by my colleague in the Florida State Department of Religion, Lawrence Cunningham. Their appearance together was a felicitous match.

"Joe Bernardin, a prelate for all the people" was my paean to the life and work of Cardinal Joseph Bernardin, archbishop of Chicago, on the occasion of his death. Bernardin was a favorite of mine long before his appointment to the Chicago archdiocese. He was one of a number of U.S. bishops who were progressive and distinctively post-Vatican II in their commitment to reform and servant leadership. Only a few of their breed remain in a U.S. hierarchy which, largely appointed by John Paul II, is much more conservative. Bernardin was a model bishop—truly a "servant of servants." An elderly priest who was a member of the Chicago archdiocese assigned to work in a Tallahassee parish, shook my hand and, with tears in his eyes thanked me for writing about "my bishop." I had tears when I re-read the article for this anthology. Joe Bernardin was a man of God.

Catholic bishops' economic ideas don't match U.S. view of wealth

"Economic Justice for All," the pastoral letter the U.S. Conference of Catholic Bishops passed overwhelmingly last November, stimulated less debate than its preliminary drafts in 1984. What the bishops have to say about the American economy does not square with the national mood. Most of us would rather not be bothered with the questions they raise.

Lawrence Cunningham reviews on this page a new book about Dorothy Day, who reminds us of the tension between traditional Roman Catholic and American notions concerning wealth and poverty. In the classic Catholic tradition, voluntary poverty is seen as spiritual virtue. When you think about it, though, taking a vow of poverty is downright un-American.

In much of our history, wealth has signaled virtue; poverty has signaled vice. The Puritan ethic, in both its religious and secularized versions, holds poverty in basic contempt. The received assumption was that one who worked hard would prosper. Those who were poor were being punished for their sins.

Added to this initial bias was the application of evolutionary thinking during the Gilded Age (1870-1900): through evolutionary struggle, the mechanism of natural selection guaranteed the success of the fittest of the species. In "Acres of Diamonds," a famous Gilded Age speech he delivered 6,000 times over 40 years, Baptist minister Russell Conwell advised, "Money is power. Every good man and woman ought to strive for power, to do good with it when obtained. I say get rich, get rich!"

Our inherited conclusion, then, is that most of the poor are, as George Bernard Shaw's Alfred Doolittle called himself, "undeserving." They are undeserving" of compassion, that is, but not undeserving of their condition. In the 1870s, Henry Ward Beecher, America's most influential pulpiteer, could say, "Looking comprehensively through city and town and village and country, the general truth will stand, that no man in this land suffers from poverty unless it be more than his fault—unless it be his SIN...There is enough and to spare thrice over; and if men have not enough, it is owning to the want of provident care, and foresight, and frugality, and wise saving."

There you have it. While it may not be a sin to be born poor in this country, it is a sin to remain poor. The biblical bias toward the poor of the land, reflected in the concerns of the eighth-century Hebrew prophets and in the Christian Gospels of Matthew and Luke, conflicts with attitudes deeply rooted in American culture. The bishops remind us that "From the Scriptures and church teaching, we learn that the justice of a society is tested by the treatment of the poor." The bishops also remind us that poverty has increased dramatically in America during the last decade: "Since 1973 the poverty rate has increased nearly a third. Although the recent recovery has brought a slight decline in the rate, it remains at a level that is higher than at almost any time during the last two decades."

The bishops do not suggest a radical solution to the problems of the U.S. economy. They recognize the legitimacy of the American heritage of a free-market, private-ownership economy. They acknowledge that capitalism promotes incentive, hope and creative activity, and increases aggregate wealth. But they also recognize that unregulated capitalism can produce fraud, monopoly and intolerable disparities in wealth.

I know even less about economics than economists. But I do know—as the bishops acknowledge—that the American economy is mixed, always has been and probably always will be. It's a mixture of public and private activity, and the only real issue is over what constitutes a balanced mix at a given time in our history. To talk about reverting to laissez-faire capitalism on the one hand, or to advocate a turn to the radical left on the other, is beside the point.

Americans, including American Catholics, may not be attuned to Catholic social teaching, but they do have an ingrained sense of fairness. It is time to think more about those who are not in the economic mainstream. Fair play requires it.

In another place, Professor Cunningham has written that "a saint is a person so grasped by a religious vision that it becomes central to his or her life in a way that radically changes the person and leads others to glimpse the value of that vision." We are all indebted to the Dorothy Days of this world, whose magnificent obsessions direct our attention to the needs of the poor. We are likewise indebted to the Catholic bishops, for admonishing us to work for a greater approximation of economic justice.

—January 17, 1987

Joe Bernardin, a prelate for all the people

Perhaps the most notable aspect of the fall meeting The National Conference of Catholic Bishops this past week was the absence of the nation's longest-serving Catholic prelate. Joseph Cardinal Bernardin, Archbishop of Chicago, served as the conference's general secretary—functionally chief of staff—from/1968 to '72, and as its president from 1974 to 77. This year, however, Bernardin was too ill to attend. Early Thursday, at age 68, he died of pancreatic cancer.

Cardinal Bernardin was a theological moderate and a social progressive who typically played the role of reconciling centrist between liberal and conservative factions in his church. He was a principal drafter of the 1983 pastoral letter on nuclear weapons, a role that put him on a *Time* cover headlined "God and the Bomb." Most recently he initiated the "Common Ground" program, a proposal to hold a series of dialogues to discuss matters that divide Catholics of both the left and right.

One of Bernardin's contributions to religious ethics is the idea of a consistent ethic of life for Catholics. He called it a "seamless garment" which he began knitting in a series of addresses in the mid-1980s.

In short, he called for a linkage of the church's "no first use" of nuclear weapons stance, its opposition to the death penalty as well as to abortion, and its advocacy for the poor and powerless. Bernardin argued that the way Catholics deal with any particular issue—abortion or capital punishment—"should be related to support for a systemic vision of life."

Some conservatives deride what they refer to as Bernardin's "seamy garment" because they think he did not differentiate between the absolutely evil and the merely undesirable. I think Benardin's approach is an imaginative and helpful way of framing the issues, though not without some problems. But it is an authentically Catholic way of doing ethics, in the tradition of Aristotelian and Thomistic moral theory.

Bernardin's leadership style was not that of the prince of the church who pronounces. He consulted and listened before acting. On his installation as Archbishop on August 25, 1983, he said to his priests, "I am Joseph, your brother." After consultation, he made hard decisions but even those of his flock who have disagreed with him appreciated the fact that he did have a consultative process.

When his health began to fail, Protestants, Jews, and secularists in the Chicago area regularly asked, "How is our Cardinal doing?" There was both sadness for, and inspiration from, this holy man who was aspiring to understand death as a friend. In his living and dying he demonstrated that seamless open integrity is more persuasive than mere authority. He said recently, "I'm glad when people tell me that I'm the same Joe Bernardin they have known for 40 years." Indeed.

—November 16, 1996

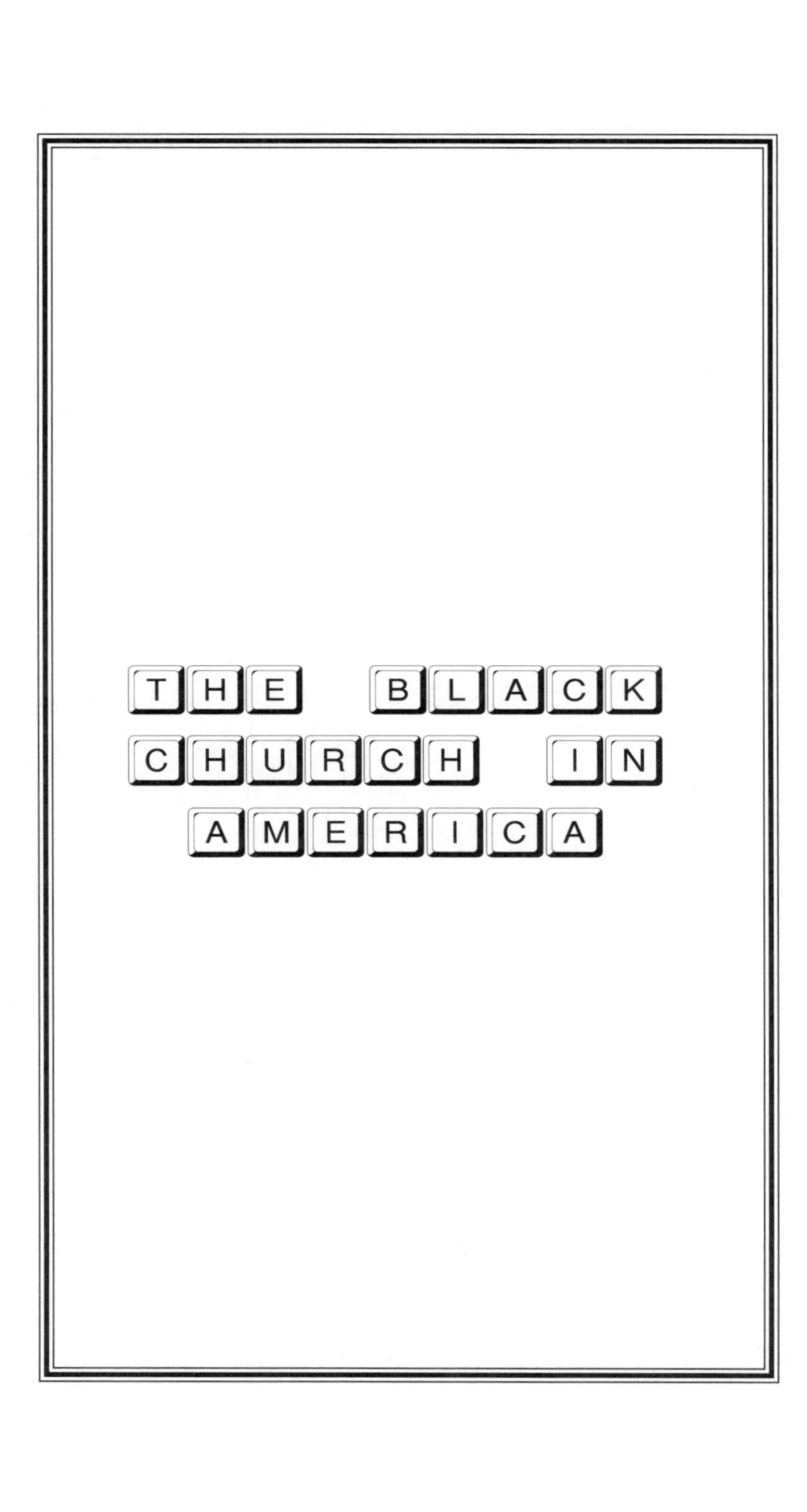
THE BLACK
CHURCH IN
AMERICA

The Black Church in America

My columns, articles and book chapters on the black church in United States history, on the persons and work of Martin Luther King, Jr. and Malcolm X, and on the civil rights—black consciousness movements could themselves constitute an anthology. They are rooted in classroom lectures and personal experiences spanning almost five decades.

The first selection, "A challenging future for the black church," is chosen because it provides a general review of the development of the black church in African-American history and culture. I refer to the late C. Eric Lincoln's and Lawrence H. Mamiya's book "The Black Church in the African-American Experience," which, at the time of this writing, is still the best single volume on the subject.

"Jews and blacks: toward resuming the conversation" was written out of an abiding concern for the rift between the black and Jewish communities that began soon after 1968. The column provided the opportunity to remember the bond between the Jewish and black communities during the early civil rights movement (1954-1965), a bond epitomized by two great American spirits: Abraham Joshua Heschel and Martin Luther King, Jr. I think Cornel West is the most influential African-American public intellectual at the turn of the century. Michael Lerner is a provocative spokesman in behalf of Jewish renewal in a pluralist culture.

"It's fitting that AME church leads the way," is commentary on the election of Vashti Murphy McKenzie as the first woman to the African Methodist Episcopal Church's episcopacy. I came to have an appreciation for the leadership role of the AME churches in the advancement of black Americans religiously, politically and culturally. It is, I observed, not coincidental that the AME church took an important symbolic step in the engagement of the "gender problem" in black religious leadership. This column might well have fit in the gender section, but it also works well here.

A challenging future for the black church

During Black History Month it is appropriate to remember the role of the black church in America. The church is the oldest and, traditionally, the central institution in black communities.

In their recent book, "The Black Church in the African-American Experience," two scholars of black religious groups, C. Eric Lincoln and Lawrence H. Mamiya, write: "Past tradition has cast the Black Church as the proverbial 'rock in a weary land'—the first and last refuge for those who call it home, and all those who live in the shadow of its promises."

On the one hand, Europeans involved in the slave trade argued that conversion of slaves to Christianity justified slavery in the Americas'; on the other hand, slave owners worried that conversion to Christianity and baptism undermined the institution of slavery. Their worries were assuaged when Colonial courts ruled that baptism did not make a black slave free. Throughout the seventeenth century there was spasmodic concern expressed by European Christian leaders for the salvation of African slaves.

In the eighteenth century, more systematic efforts to convert African-Americans were attempted. While these efforts bore some fruit, it wasn't until the religious revivals of the 1740s—the Great Awakening—that large numbers of slaves were converted. The conversion experience of evangelical Christianity probably was identified with the African notion of spirit possession. Singing spirituals, dancing in a counterclockwise circle (the "ring shout"), and approximating the rhythms of the drum, the slaves in a sense converted European Christianity to African styles as much as they themselves were converted to the slavemaster's religion.

From the Christian faith of the slaves there emerged what is frequently called "the invisible institution," the black church in the antebellum South. The church was invisible because it was not formally recognized by ecclesiastical authorities. As an ex-slave put it: "The colored folks had their code of religion, not nearly so complicated as the white man's religion, but more closely observed...When we had our own meetings of this kind, we held them in our own way and were not interfered with by white folks."

Meanwhile, institutional churches—visible institutions—of free blacks developed in the North. African Baptists churches were organized in Philadelphia, Boston, and New York from 1804 to 1809. Richard Allen and his associates established the African Methodist Episcopal Church in 1816 at Philadelphia. Other denominations of black Methodists were formed during this period. These churches became the central institutions for communities of free blacks in the North. From the beginning their ministries had cultural, economic, social and political components. It is instructive to note that the first national black political organization was convened in Philadelphia's Bethel AME-Church in 1830, an organization to address the issue of slavery.

Most historians of American religion typically depict the growth of the black church after emancipation as "a merger between the invisible institution of the slave South and the independent churches of the North." One point on which there is virtual consensus is that it was the central institution in the life of the African-American during the last four decades of the nineteenth century. In the wake of the failure of Reconstruction and in the face of recalcitrant American racism, the church was the only institution African-Americans controlled. As historian E. Franklin Frazier put it, the church was the black person's "refuge in a hostile white world."

In the 20th century the black church has continued to respond to new challenges. Early in the century, holiness and then pentecostal groups joined the Baptists and Methodists as a third force in African-American religion. The Church of God in Christ emerged as the largest black Pentecostal denomination.

When African-Americans emigrated to the urban centers two new versions of the black church developed: large, institutional churches and "storefront churches." An example of the former is the Abyssinian Baptist Church in Harlem. The storefront churches provided a more intimate sense of community than the large institutional congregations.

The role of the black church in the civil rights movement, 1954-1966, was pivotal. It is no accident that the major leader of the battle for racial justice was a black Baptist minister. In this case the black religious leadership was able to fashion a coalition of Protestant, Eastern Orthodox, Roman Catholic and Jewish Americans in behalf of civil rights.

The story of the black church provides its people with what a historian once called a "usable past," that is, a sense of the past with which it can meet the future.

—February 20, 1993

Jews and blacks: toward resuming the conversation

An indelible memory from Civil Rights Movement events in 1964-65 is that of a bearded rabbi, my picture of an eighth-century Hebrew prophet, striding down the street. He was arm in arm with Greek Orthodox primate Archbishop Iakovos, with Roman Catholic priests, with labor leader Walter Reuther and Martin Luther King, Jr. Rabbi Abraham Joshua Heschel wrote of his marching with King in Selma: "I felt as if my legs were praying."

My consciousness of King's holiday and Black History Month has been augmented this year by the observance of the 25th *yahrzeit* (anniversary of the death) of Rabbi Heschel. As a graduate student, I considered him second only to King as an influence in shaping my personal and professional aspirations; as a professor who focuses on religion in the United States, I am among those who count Heschel as the nation's most significant 20th-century Jewish theologian. Hundreds of events have been scheduled to commemorate his life and work in the weeks ahead.

Heschel and King together is not just a construction of my memory. They were together. They marched, prayed and deliberated together. They spoke from the biblical prophetic tradition in strikingly similar ways. In that fateful year 1968, King was keynote speaker at a gathering of rabbis convened to honor Heschel on his 60th birthday. Ten days later, Heschel spoke at King's funeral.

Heschel was no anomaly. There were many Jews who participated in the movement, several of whom were martyred to the cause of racial justice. But soon after 1968 there were growing patterns of conflict between the African-American and Jewish communities. Some African-American intellectuals, along with black political and religious leaders, have accused Jews of being heavily involved in the oppression of their people. Some Jewish intellectuals—notably those identified as neoconservatives—have argued that many of the public policies championed by African Americans are antithetical to Jewish interests.

Among a number of items of unfinished business at century's end is serious dialogue between Jews and African Americans. Get set for a recommendation—*Jews and Blacks: A Dialogue on Race, Religion, and Culture in America*, by Michael Lerner and Cornel West.

Lerner is the author of *Jewish Renewal: A Path to Healing and Transformation*, and the editor of *Tikkun*, a bimonthly journal of religious, literary, political and cultural criticism. West, the author of a number of books, including the best-selling *Race Matters*, is a professor of Afro-American studies and the philosophy of religion at Harvard University. The book is based on taped conversations between Lerner and West. While it is uneven, it is a good start toward serious conversation. The book, interestingly enough, is dedicated "to the legacies of Martin Luther King, Jr. and Abraham Joshua Heschel" and to the authors' sons, Clifton West and Akiba Lerner. It is a tough conversation dealing with painful issues. But these two public intellectuals believe that honest conversation can "imaginatively project an all-embracing moral vision for the future." This dialogue, among others, is desirable for both Jews and blacks. And for those of us who are neither.

—February 21, 1998

It's fitting that AME Church leads the way

This week's election of the Rev. Vashti Murphy McKenzie to the episcopacy of the African Methodist Episcopal Church proved newsworthy but not all that surprising. The first woman bishop in the history of the AME Church and the highest-ranking officer of her sex in any black denomination is as historically appropriate as it is a welcome milestone.

The AME Church began in 1787 when Richard Allen, Absalom Jones and other black worshippers withdrew from the St. George Methodist Episcopal Church in Philadelphia. Allen, Jones and William White were requested to leave their pews while kneeling in a section of the church they did not know was closed to black Christians. As Allen explained it, "All went out of the church in a body and they were no more plagued with [us] in that church."

Allen was born a slave in Philadelphia in 1760. He was sold to a Delaware planter. He was converted and became a Methodist in 1777, and soon thereafter was allowed to purchase his freedom. He became a Methodist preacher in 1780 and received ministerial appointments from Bishop Francis Asbury. He left the white-controlled Methodist Episcopal Church because of racial discrimination rather than doctrinal differences.

Allen then became bishop of the independent AME church, an institution that constituted the first successful black "stride toward freedom"—secular or religious—in North American history. It was not accidental that the birth of the first black denomination occurred in Philadelphia, the most multicultural and progressive city in the nation's late colonial-early republican period.

One of the important stories in African-American history is that of the influence of northern black churches, composed of free citizens. From the beginning the AME church and most of the other Methodist and Baptist bodies that followed in its wake were interested in providing social services for those in need. The AME Church in particular emphasized education in the interests of supporting a trained ministry and in advancing African Americans. The Rev. McKenzie's election, therefore, is in continuity with an established liberation tradition.

Her election also constitutes the welcome engagement of one of the black church's most obvious problems: Leadership in black churches has remained largely a male preserve. The facts support the generalization that even though the black church's successes would have been impossible without the support of women, the offices of preacher and pastor have been withheld from them. The adage is that the pulpit has been viewed as "men's space," the pew as "women's place." McKenzie, who is pastor of Payne Memorial AME Church in Baltimore, reportedly is "a dynamic preacher and community organizer." After her election she told delegates to the General Conference in Cincinnati, "The stained glass ceiling has been pierced and broken." She acknowledged, "I stand here tonight on the shoulders of the unordained women who serve without affirmation or appointment." Indeed.

So the AME church pioneers once again. The denomination that led the engagement of racial discrimination in North American churches now leads the engagement of gender discrimination in black churches. Let us hope other black church groups follow its lead.

—July 15, 2000

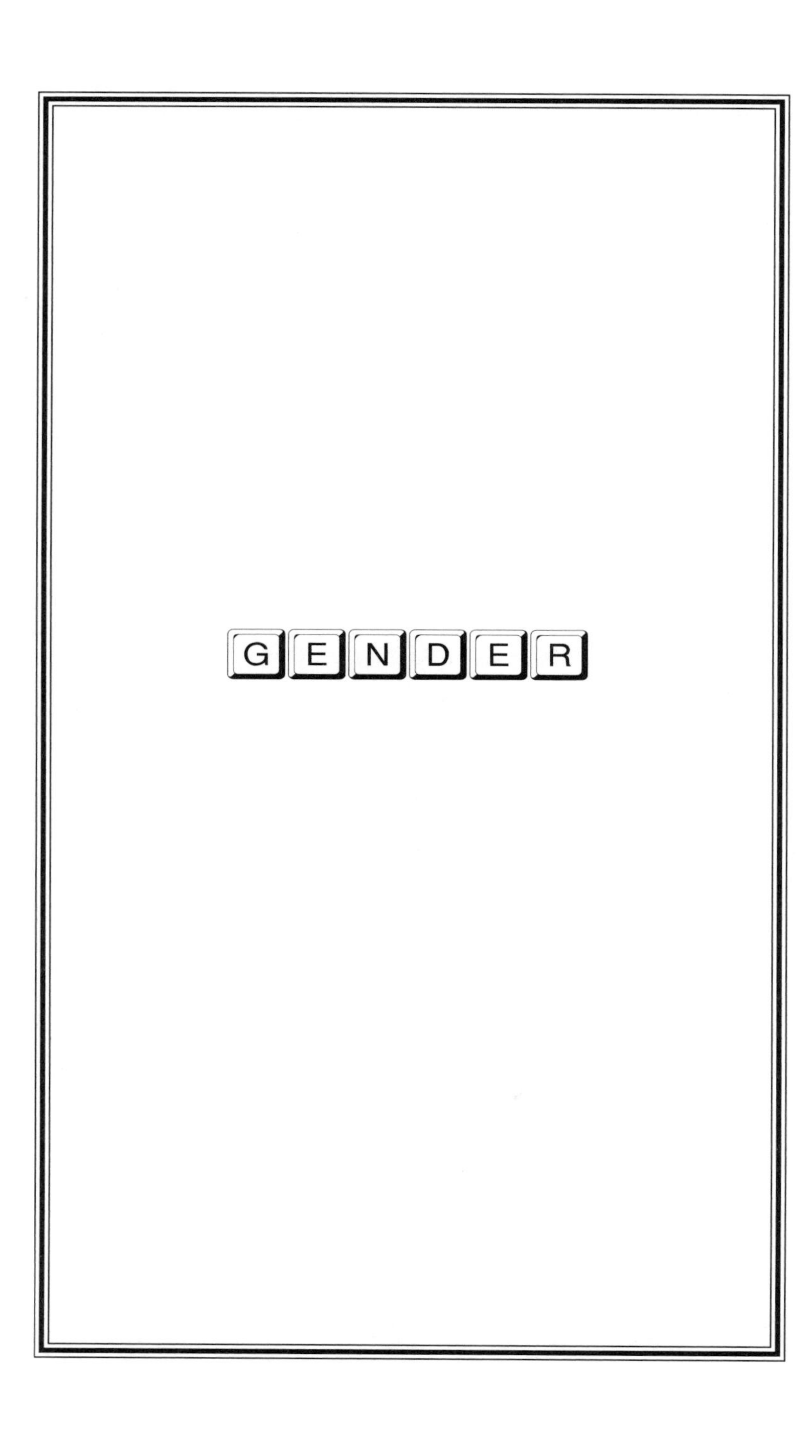
GENDER

Gender

A new interest in women in religious thought and the role of women in American religious life are among the most interesting stories in American religion the past thirty years. I reckon that I am a feminist. I certainly have been influenced by feminist scholarship from both the religious studies and the American Studies sides of my academic work. A course I offered, "Women in American Religion and Culture," was one of the products of this influence. In this section perhaps the second selection logically should come first. To arrange them chronologically is admittedly arbitrary.

"Sophia is not everyone's choice" is a play on the title of William Styron's 1979 novel *Sophie's Choice.* Much ado was made about a 1993 ecumenical women's "Re-Imagining" conference which dealt with, among other topics, the female personification of God. Two retired Methodist bishops feared that these "pitiable" women were modifying "the doctrine of God to the degree that the feminine principle is made a part of the Godhead." Perhaps I should make the shameless confession that, for many years, I have thought of the Holy Spirit as female in character. With the Moravian leader who ironically had great influence on the shaping of Methodist belief and piety, Count Nikolaus Ludwig von Zizendorf (1700-60), I address the Holy Spirit as "Mother." After reading the conference's proceedings I judged it an interesting convocation.

"Including her story: women in religion" is a general review of the rise of consciousness concerning the recognition of women's contributions to religious belief and practices in North American religious groups. Already the 1994 column is quite dated as feminist scholarship moves forward and as women assume greater visibility, attaining more leadership positions in American religious life.

Sophia is not everyone's choice

The fur has been flying in several old line Protestant denominations as a result of a women's ecumenical "Re-Imagining" conference held Nov. 4-7, 1993, in Minneapolis. The turbulence is particularly tense in the United Methodist Church, the Presbyterian Church (USA), and the Evangelical Lutheran Church in America. The conference was planned in conjunction with the World Council of Churches' "Ecumenical Decade of Churches in Solidarity with Women."

The ostensible reason for attacks upon the conference was the focus of much of its liturgy and discussion on the female personification of God—"Sophia," a biblical name derived from the Hebrew wisdom tradition. Wisdom, "*hochma*" in Hebrew, *"sophia"* in Greek is a female personification in the Book of Proverbs: "Does not wisdom call, and does not understanding raise her voice?" She is present at creation (Proverbs 8:22-31), beside Yahweh "like a master worker." The Reimagining Conference was hardly a coming-out party for Sophia or a press release introducing a new-age goddess: Jewish and Christian thinkers have for centuries spoken and written of Sophia as an attribute or personification of God, sometimes as a metaphor for God.

Conservative critics are charging heresy. Denominational bureaucrats are signaling a siege mentality. Retired Methodist Bishop Earl G. Hunt has stated that "No comparable heresy has appeared in the church in the last 15 centuries." His counterpart, Bishop William R. Cannon, a former dean of the Candler School of Theology, finds it pitiable that women feel they must "modify the doctrine of God to the degree that the feminine principle is made a part of the Godhead" to advance their cause. Influential Presbyterian, (USA) pastors are publicly expressing no confidence in the denomination's General Assembly Council for contributing to the conference's funding and defending Presbyterian participation in it. The controversy could cost the Presbyterian Church $2.5 million in contributions.

Listening to tapes of the conference I heard uneven attempts to inquire into interpretations of the person and work of Jesus, into the meaning of community, human sexuality, family, and church based on women's biological, social and spiritual experiences. Womanist theologian Delores Williams, for instance, gave a thoughtful interpretation of Jesus' life from the standpoint of the African American woman's socially ascribed roles. The affirmation of women's sexuality in the infamous milk-and-honey ritual was a tasteful integration of those two elements so long divided in Western religion: the erotic and the spiritual. Prayers to Sophia were not meant to replace conventional images of God, but rather to broaden and deepen those images.

There are a number of non-male images of deity in the Bible. So what's the fuss? The standard feminist answer is that exclusively male metaphors for God legitimize patriarchal oppression: "If God is male, then males are God." Beyond this obvious answer, I think that male terms for God have served as a sexual cloak. When you introduce female metaphors for deity, not only gender but sexuality becomes more blatant. The fears and resistance to (despite the fascination with) such open acknowledgment of sexuality are deeply rooted. Such fundamental reimagining is jarring but healthy.

In the meantime, please note that those who cooked and served millions of church suppers, raised many millions of dollars, and taught millions of church school classes are increasingly co-equals with men in many of our churches and synagogues. They will continue to find voice and space to support and challenge each other. We are all going to be the better for their initiatives.

—May 28, 1994

Including her story: women in religion

Perhaps the most radical revolution that has occurred in religious life and thought in the United States and Canada in the past three decades is the gender revolution. I use the term radical in its basic meaning: to the roots! Women's studies in religion have contributed to the recovery of "Her Story"-women in the symbolization of religious traditions; the use of religious authority to legitimatize women's subordination in society and culture; and women's roles in religious communities and institutions.

Women's studies scholars have challenged the identification of male with human in religion, arguing that this assumption is the root of patriarchal bias, particularly in Judaism and Christianity. They have gone even further in critical analysis of the assumption that the divine is to be imaged in exclusively male terms. A number of women theologians have broadened and deepened traditional understandings of divinity, salvation, freedom, and justice.

Feminist scholars have also demonstrated the linkage between religious assumptions concerning gender relations and women's status in other social institutions. Throughout much of our history, religious authority has been cited as the ultimate legitimator of patriarchy. It is rather obvious that issues of gender and value are inextricably related in culture. Feminist professor of religion Mary Daly states it well in an oft-quoted passage from her book,

Beyond God the Father: "If God in 'his' heaven is a father ruling 'his' people, then it is in the nature of things and according to divine plan...that society be male dominated."

In the last quarter of the 20th century women have moved toward parity in mainline religious groups. Today most mainline Protestant churches in North America ordain women. Reform, Conservative and Reconstructionist Jewish bodies ordain women rabbis. The result is that perhaps as much as 10 percent of the clergy in the United States and Canada are women. One in three seminarians are women. The Untied Methodist Church, the Episcopal Church and the Evangelical Lutheran Church in America have at least one woman bishop.

Aside from the big story, there has been the recovery of many subsidiary stories—"her stories" along the way. The work of Protestant evangelical women in 19th-century America and their initiative in behalf of women's rights and other social issues comes to mind. In the early decades of this century, women had shared more equal status in Holiness and Pentecostal traditions, faith communities that tended to emphasize co-equality under the leadership of the Holy Spirit. We are only beginning to appreciate the stories of Roman Catholic nuns and their awesome contribution to the building of schools, hospitals, and service organizations. The essential leadership of Ellen White among the Seventh-Day Adventists, Phoebe Palmer in the Holiness movement, and Mother Ann Lee with her Shaker followers are at last receiving the attention they deserve.

Journalist Mary Tabor writes of hearing Episcopal Bishop Jane Holmes Dixon illustrating our unwillingness to accept God's grace by a personal experience she had when she was sick. A friend offered to help by taking the Dixon children while their mother, Jane, recuperated. The friend also insisted on washing the family's dirty clothes. Instead of accepting graciously, Jane Dixon protested. One parishioner, a 69-year-old woman, nudged a reporter sitting next to her. "A man couldn't tell a story like that," she whispered. "He's always had somebody to wash his clothes."

The story is becoming more complete and symmetrical as Her Story is included.

—March 18, 1995

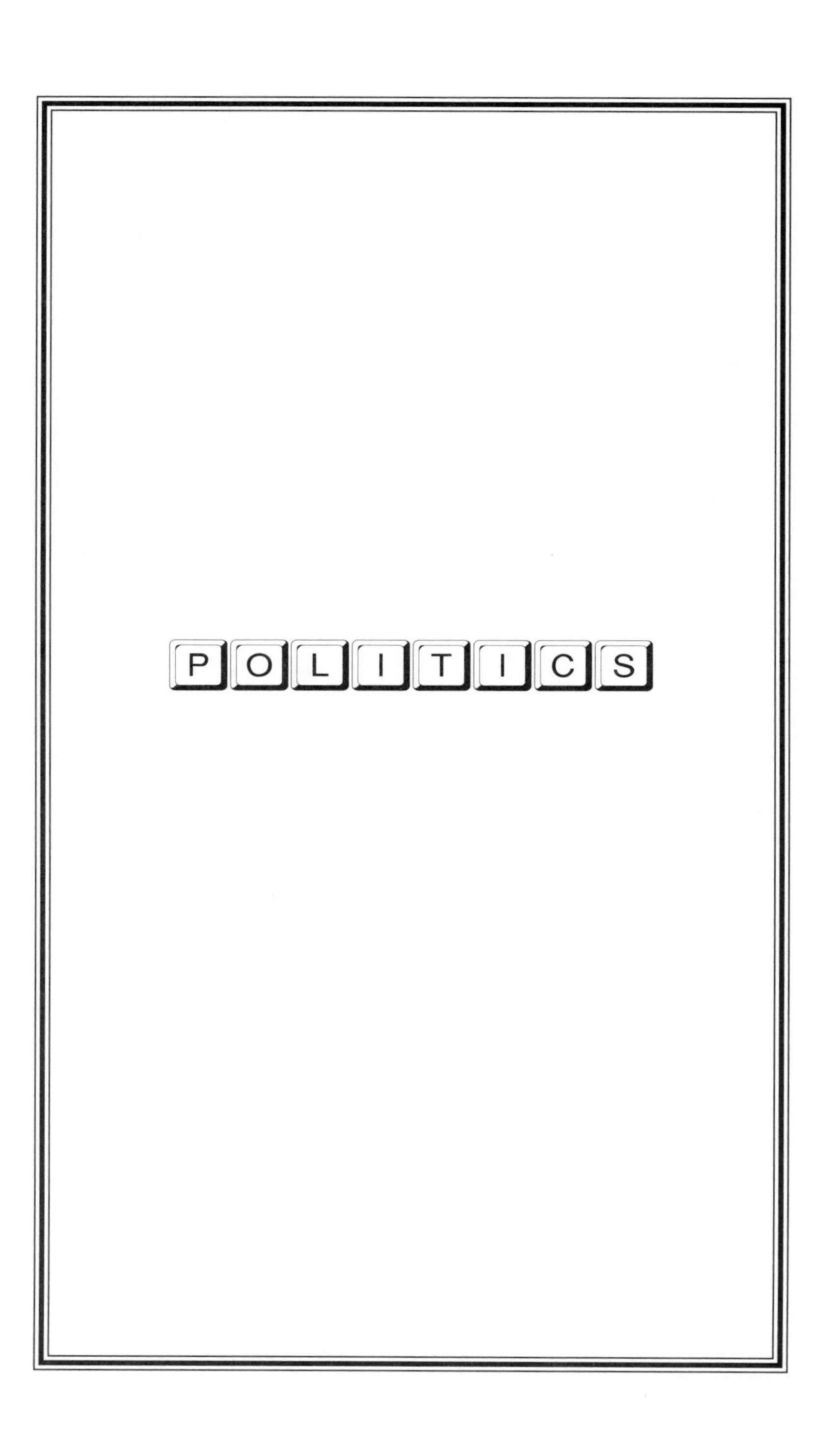
POLITICS

Politics

Of the mixing of religion and politics there has been much in *Religion in America.* This has been their strength for some readers according to their comments to *Tallahassee Democrat* editors and to me. For others the mix has proved perplexing, sometimes infuriating. I can't help myself. Perhaps it is a mischievous rebellion that goes back to my teenage career as a butcher boy in a meat market whose manager instructed me to avoid all and any discussion of religion and politics. Actually it is the conviction that religion and politics are so inextricably linked that leads me to discuss the intersection of the two realms. I have chosen to include two columns on President Clinton in this section rather than create a separate Clinton section.

"Of political religion and religious politics" is a column in which I first used the typologies of "political religion" and "religious politics." I found them to be helpful clarifying concepts and used them often, explicitly or implicitly, in subsequent columns.

"Religious politicians: stop whining" was directed at those politically mobilized religious leaders and the followers who tend to cry "religious intolerance" when others disagree with them. The column was carried by a number of newspapers. Many persons expressed their agreement.

There also was considerable reader response, both public and private, to my column "Obviously he does not feel our pain," in response to President Clinton's August 17, 1998 "I misled the American people speech." I almost didn't write "yet another" interpretation of the Clinton drama, but I am glad I did. Some knowledgeable types who read the major papers daily gave it high marks. "Clinton and Lewinsky: the irony of it all" was my last "Clinton" column. I wrote many columns about the Clintons, the fact that these two are the only ones included in the anthology perhaps reflects the sad consequences of a side-tracked presidency.

Of religious politics and political religion

Politics is the way things get done in human affairs. Every political or economic question has an ethical and religious dimension. So it is natural for religious groups to participate in the discussion of public issues.

That participation produces two hybrids: "political religion," in which religious groups engage in heavy political mobilization; and "religious politics," in which politicians or political parties use religious leaders or groups to rally support for themselves and their programs.

When religious groups become too politicized, though, or political parties become too closely identified with sectarian religion, both religious and political integrity are compromised.

ITEM: In a letter to other pastors written on his congregation's letterhead, a mainline Tallahassee pastor endorsed the candidacy of one of his flock. "He has exhibited a strong Christian influence in his business life, in community affairs...I therefore recommend that you..." His opponent was also a devout churchman with a reputation for honesty and many years of public service. Is a voter supposed to decide which candidate would be the most Christian legislator?

ITEM: "Bob Graham is 'an extreme liberal, (with a) New Deal socialist view of government, (who) believes in a large government bureaucracy fed by high taxes." Graham went to "a liberal Ivy League institution, has strong political ties with liberal Washington and East Coast Democrats," and "a sister-in-law who runs a left-wing newspaper: The *Washington Post*." Paula Hawkins, in comparison; "is consistently conservative in many areas, including biblical values, foreign policy, constitution, etc." This evaluation was offered by the Florida Christians for Good Government. I'll spare you what the newsletter said about Steve Pajcic (Democratic candidate for governor).

ITEM: Jerry Draper, former president of the Southern Baptist Convention, endorses Pat Robertson's candidacy with this proclamation: "America is to be a biblical republic that offers religious freedom to all but that does not deny its theistic base."

Religious leaders have found that political involvement can be a bruising experience. Jerry Falwell is vowing never to support another candidate as he did Ronald Reagan because it is "too polarizing to unbelievers. We're going back to where we were before Moral Majority, when we had a clear purpose but did not have a major emphasis on politics."

Soon after Falwell called Bishop Desmond Tutu a phony and advocated support for former Philippine President Ferdinand Marcos, his political platform collapsed. He was left swinging in the breeze without much aid from his political allies in the Reagan administration.

Billy Graham, the unofficial White House chaplain in the 1950s and again in the late 1960s, suffered personal and public pain for his close ties with, and personal endorsement of, Richard Nixon. Don't look for Graham to become partisan again.

Politicians and political parties, in their exploitation of religious leaders and groups, can themselves end up exploitees.

ITEM: The eagerness of the GOP to integrate the religious right into its new Republican majority has drawbacks when one notes that many of the younger Republican voters are economic conservatives but social libertines. Frank Fahrenkkopf, chairman of the Republican National Committee, has to have mixed feelings about Pat Robertson's candidacy.

ITEM: Jesse Jackson's self-promotion does little for Democratic Party cohesiveness or for genuine black political development. Whatever his candidacy does for Jackson himself, or ostensibly for black Americans, it is hardly a plus for Democrat restoration.

ITEM: The readiness of political leaders, who are noted for neither their personal piety nor their church loyalty, to attend prayer breakfasts and sit on crusade platforms is transparent to all but the most gullible citizens.

Politicians and clergy should practice restraint. Clergy, like journalists and academicians, should resist being seduced by the trappings of power and allowing themselves to get too cozy with politicians. Catholic bishops and televangelists alike probably should stop short of opposing or endorsing particular candidates. Politicians should be prudent in their use of any religious faction in forging their coalitions. Inauthentic expressions of piety or rhetorical excess are not without peril.

A disclaimer: I write as one who is neither politically nor religiously indifferent. Active participation in the political process should stem from ethical and religious convictions. There is no substitute for our supporting candidates up front, early on and unequivocally. That is the only way the system can work. But when supporting a candidate or pleading a cause, one shouldn't claim to be chairing the Lord's own political-action committee.

—November 15, 1986

Religious politicians: stop whining

One function of religious groups in the United States is to participate in the shaping of what the late Walter Lippman called "the public philosophy." That is, faith communities often try to influence answers to the enduring question: "how are we to order our common life?" From the colonial "Election Day Sermons" to the activities of the Christian Coalition, such has it ever been.

Only a few flat-footed secularists argue that religious groups do not have the right to argue politics in the public square. But when religious groups become political, there are a few rules they ought to accept as part of the process:

1. When others disagree with you on questions of values and policy, don't cry "bigotry."

To disagree with specific political positions of the Christian Right, the Catholic bishops, or mainline religious liberals, for that matter, should not be equated with Christian or Catholic bashing. A number of Christian Coalition leaders in general, and Pat Robertson in particular, should understand that it's not their religious convictions that most of their critics are engaging. It's their political convictions.

Again, no serious commentator argues with the right of the Catholic bishops to get tough in their opposition to abortion coverage in health plans. But American Catholics must understand that it is possible for others to respect both their church and its right to witness, and yet feel free to disagree with the teaching authority—the Magisterium—of the hierarchy.

2. Assume a procedural co-equality among the various voices in the political arena.

However convinced religious groups may be about the absolute rightness of their position, they should recognize the legitimacy and good faith of other groups. They should neither demonize nor dismiss the opposition. Columnist Cal Thomas demonstrated either supreme arrogance or ignorance (or both) in his July 10 column, printed in *The Democrat.* Thomas wrote, "For most of this century, the Christian Church has been in self-imposed exile. ....then it re-emerged on the scene in the 1980s."

How parochial. In the first place, Thomas equates "The Church" with conservative evangelicals who did indeed become politically mobilized in the 1980s. There are, however, other types of Christians. In the second place, he apparently dismisses every incident of religiously inspired social and political action in the other seven decades of the 20th century, everything from the Social Creed of the Federal Council of Churches in 1908 to mainline participation in the civil-rights movement of the 1950s and 1960s. His reference to the "Pagan Left," finally, is just as demeaning as some of the epithets used to disparage the Christian Right.

3. Assume the responsibility for your own inconsistencies and excesses.

To venture into the public arena is to expose oneself and one's cause to the astringent light of public scrutiny, both by the media and by one's opponents. One can't have it both ways. You have to learn to take it. Every movement, furthermore, has its crazies. Either distance yourself from them or be vulnerable to their excesses. You can't negotiate with the crazies. Sometimes you can contain them; more often they will cripple you.

In a word, step up to the plate and take your cut at the ball. But don't expect your opponents to roll over. Above all, quit whining.

—July 30, 1994

Obviously, he does not feel our pain

I feel sheepish writing about *L'Affaire* when there are more important affairs about which to write. Like many of you, I say that I am tired of hearing about Bill and Monica, Ken and Linda—yet I am attentive every time another shoe falls in our protracted national soap.

So here comes one more comment on Clinton's performance 12 days ago. I have a hunch that events from this point on will be anticlimactic. The story will grind on, but the president probably has lost the opportunity to turn anything around. So what's this got to do with religion?

Outward religious dimensions were manifest as President and Mrs. Clinton attended the Foundry United Methodist Church in Washington the day before his testimony to the grand jury. Foundry's pastor, interestingly enough, is J. Philip Wogaman, a former professor of social ethics. But these are the trappings of religion; they provide photo opportunities and gestures to cover "the religion thing."

The consensus among the pundits, politicians and public intellectuals is that Clinton's address was abysmal because it lacked contrition, a declaration of repentance and a confessional apology to those he had hurt. Note the religious character of these words.

Those such as Yale law professor Stephen Carter, who expressed disappointment at the lack of contrition and repentance, should understand that Clinton was not dealing in moral or religious concepts. His rhetoric was legal and political in character, consistent with his posture since January. His attitude was more sullen, and his trimming and spinning were more obvious than usual.

Clinton's argument that even presidents have private lives, that "it's nobody's business but ours," is only a half-truth. When he publicly denied the allegation of an affair that took place not on private property but in the White House, the affair became increasingly public.

He seems oblivious to the fact that, these days, none of us enjoy the possibility of privacy we once did. Especially not presidents. If anyone decides to really investigate us, there is no hiding. Even private confession becomes a public procedure as we witness Jesse Jackson (Billy Graham's apparent replacement as the White House chaplain of record) providing updates on the spiritual status of each of the Clintons.

Supporting the Clintons has proved costly for many who have been part of the team. Aside from Hillary and Chelsea, there are members of his staff and Cabinet to whom he lied who are now dangling in the wind, many strapped with attorney fees. He needs to apologize and to ask for forgiveness.

I think the president owes Monica Lewinsky and her family an apology for an affair that lasted 18 months and was apparently characterized by infatuation and mutual expressions of affection. Regarding his attitude toward women with whom he has been involved, the old word "cad" comes to mind.

He should ask forgiveness from those of us who voted for him twice, choosing to think that his policy agenda was more important than his philandering. He has hurt the cause of decently progressive government for years to come and undermined the very office to which he aspired since adolescence. Yet he doesn't seem to get it. Perhaps his most profound lie is that he feels our pain.

—August 29, 1998

Clinton and Lewinsky: The irony of it all

Pathetic. Slogging through the Starr report tempts one to use pathos as a guiding principle of interpretation. Starr's take-no-hostages narrative does indeed reveal a pathetic adolescent clumsiness in the Clinton-Lewinsky affair. Furtive clutching in a windowless hall, a side office, the presidential bathroom.

But in truly pathetic situations, the participants do not bear primary responsibility for their plight, and neither the president nor Monica Lewinsky was an innocent victim of untoward circumstances. Both operated with a significant measure of freedom and intentionality.

Tragedy doesn't work, either. Pure tragedy entails a noble suffering or even dying in behalf of some great good—an unavoidable collision of values and power that evokes admiration or pity of a heroic protagonist. Although the president at times compares his situation to that of tragic heroes, there is no evidence of any absolute center of value around which his person and work revolve. Clinton's self apparently is infinitely reinventable, his values always negotiable. When interpreting Monica Lewinsky's thoughts and actions, nobility and a centered consciousness do not come to mind.

While there are elements of tragedy and pathos in this scandal, an ironic squint may be our best way of interpreting it. Fifty years ago, the Christian theologian Reinhold Niebuhr observed that irony often is the most appropriate standpoint from which to understand human affairs. Irony,

Niebuhr argued, involves an element of comedy. Incongruity.

Kenneth Starr is a Church of Christ rational literalist when it comes to the New Testament. It is ironic that one who claims to interpret the law in much the same way writes such an unrestrained and salacious report. Did we need to know about the cigar? Starr manifests what Niebuhr described as "the fanaticism of all good men who do not know that they are not as good as they esteem themselves."

It is likewise ironic that Clinton the spinmeister, the convincing one so good with words, is talking himself into a corner where virtually no one is taking seriously what he says. It is hard to balance fury and hatred of one's foes with contrition and repentance. Some of us feel more the voyeur watching his pious maneuvers than his sexual ones. But we'll keep watching.

A good case can be made that the biblical perspective is closer to irony than to tragedy or pathos. At least up to the belief in ultimate redemption in the sweet by and by. In the nasty here and now, the Bible interprets God as the divine judge "who laughs at human pretensions without being hostile to human aspirations." The divine laughter tends to be the word of judgment; the judgment can be transmuted into grace if we contritely recognize our vanity and repent.

On Thursday, columnist Albert Hunt wrote, "Little if any good will come out of the Clinton-Lewinsky scandal." Wrong. We're going to learn some things from this, and the system will survive. While the process continues, the ironist assumes that, just as things are never as good as they seem, neither are they as bad as they seem.

—September 19, 1998

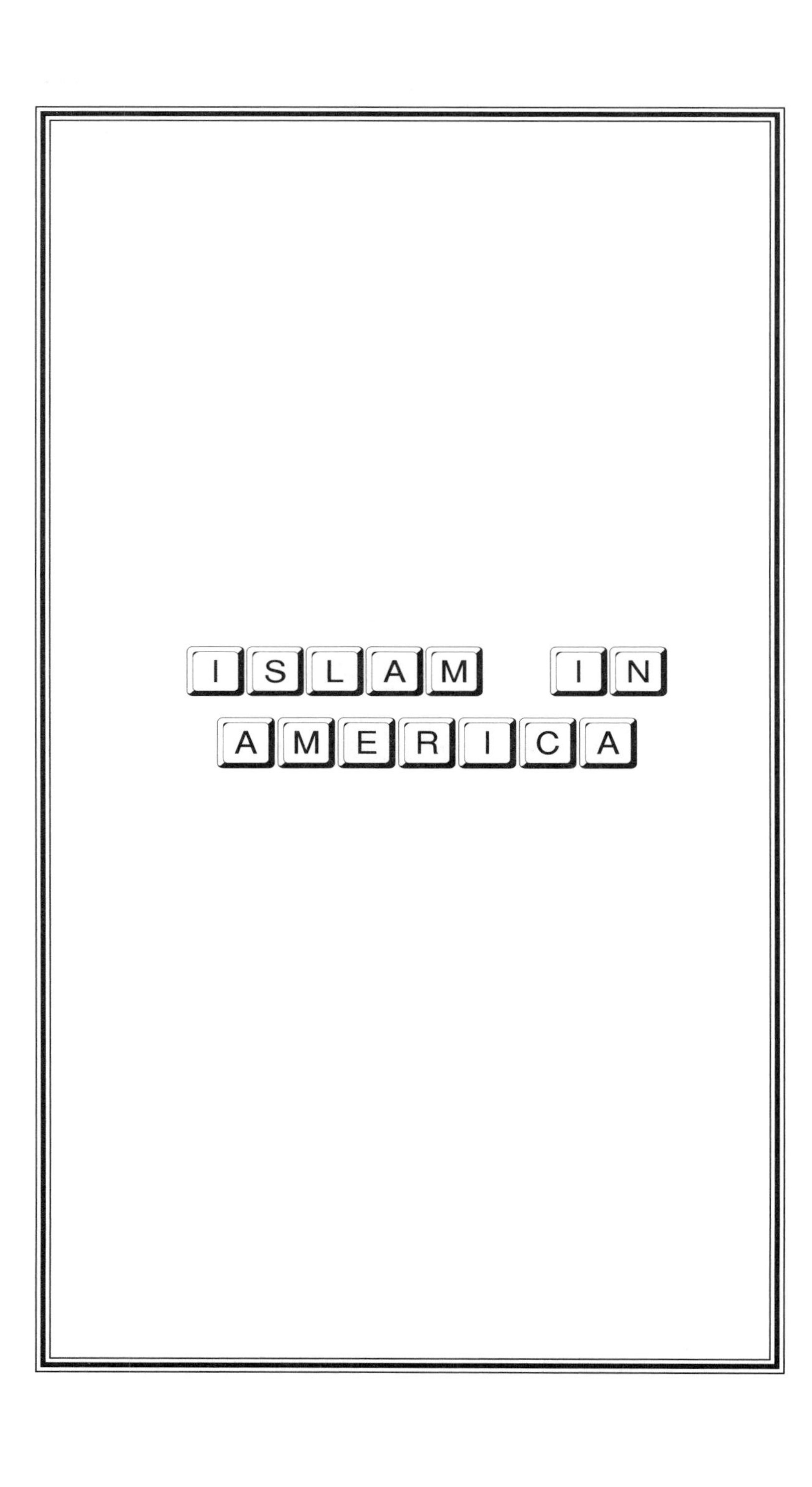
ISLAM IN
AMERICA

Islam in America

Islam in America was not a common theme in the columns, but it was included. As the second largest faith tradition in the United States it is important. Since September 11, 2001 it is of paramount importance that we understand Islam.

On the one hand, "African-American religion and the Islamic connection" could have been placed in the Black Church section. On the other hand, the largest racial-ethnic component of Muslims in the United States are African-Americans. Then too, as an Americanist who was privileged to meet and watch Malcolm X early on, I have known more about Black Muslims in this nation in particular, than about Islam in general. I have no knowledge of Arabic and the world history of Islam has not been a significant academic focus in my work. So the "Islamic connection" column does not stretch my competence and it has proved to be useful information for a number of readers and for my undergraduate students in "Religion in America" classes.

"Shedding light on the face of Islam in America" appeared in the wake of the September 11 attacks and was my attempt to describe what is generally known about Muslim life in the United States and to provide a context that might discourage anti-Islamic backlash.

African-American religion and the Islamic connection

Any observance of Black History Month on the religion page is incomplete without some consideration of

Muslims. Most American born Muslims are from the African-American population. And their influence on African-American religious and cultural consciousness has been disproportionate to their numbers.

The roots of Islam in the African-American experience technically go deeper than slavery. The first identifiable African Muslim in North America, interestingly enough to us Floridians, was one Estevan, a Moroccan guide and interpreter who came to Florida from Spain in 1527 with the Panfilo de Narvaez expedition.

The first significant Muslim presence in North America, however, was constituted by Africans brought here as slaves. As much as 20 percent of the slave population on the large plantations may have been Muslim. But the influence of Islam during slavery was not sustained.

It was not until the 20th century that Islam emerged as a significant movement among those who were part of the great black migrations to urban centers. The first significant Muslim movement among urban African-Americans was led by Timothy Drew (1886-1929), whose name was changed to Noble Drew Ali. Ali founded the Moorish Science Temple of America in 1913. After Ali's death, the temple disintegrated into several factions, one of which was the Nation of Islam. Master Wali Fard was the mysterious founder of the Nation in or around 1930, and the Honorable Elijah Muhammed led the Nation from 1934 to 1975.

In the 1960s and early 1970s, the Nation of Islam provided a counterpoint to the civil rights movement's emphasis on integrating African-Americans into mainstream American systems. The Black Muslims, as they were known, probably were the primary source of the black consciousness movement. It emphasized pride in blackness; black separation; the necessity to know black history; black unity; and black control of African-American political and economic institutions.

Since the death of Elijah Muhammed, his son, Imam Warith Deen Muhammed, has led most of the African-American Muslims into orthodox Sunni Islam. The movement changed its name to the American Muslim Mission. This radical reformation led to secession by Louis Farrakhan in 1977. Farrakhan wanted to restore Elijah Muhammed's Lost-Found Nation of Islam in the Wilderness of North America. The American Muslim Mission has approximately 100,000 members, Farrakhan's Nation of Islam around 20,000.

Black Muslims always have been a counter point to black Christianity, the "slave-master's religion." At times their message has been particularly appealing to men. Their militant black nationalism is attractive to those who want to be proactive in behalf of racial justice. Malcolm X has become a major cultural hero among African-Americans. There is something of a macho element symbolized by Muslim sports heroes such as Muhammed Ali and Kareem Abdul-Jabbar.

The Nation of Islam probably has an edge in prophetic daring. After all, it was Louis Farrakhan, not black Christian clergy, who put together the 1995 Million Man March. Muslim success in prison and inner-city ministries is impressive. Still, the Muslims probably are fated to remain the goading minority in African-American religion. The churches have the music.

—February 27, 1999

Shedding light on the face of Islam in America

Sharon, Mass. was the town down the road where, in the late 1950s, I used to take my Congregationalist youth group to the local synagogue. The rabbi at Temple Israel would introduce Protestant teen-agers to Jewish faith and worship. More than half of the town's population is Jewish.

Sharon, in south suburban Boston, is now also the home of The Islamic Center for New England. When the center moved there in the early 1990s, Temple Israel's rabbi called a meeting of the local clergy association, which voted a unanimous welcome to the new Muslims. "Sharon Welcomes Islamic Center," announced the local paper.

I've received a number of inquiries from community groups seeking speakers for presentations on Islam. So I've been brokering: linking representatives of the Muslim community with program committee chairs. Apparently it's a needed service. Twelve hours before writing this column I listened to the coarseness of a Bill O'Reilly interview with two American Muslim leaders, looked at a bigoted cartoon by Signe Wilkinson and read an outrageous column by Cal Thomas.

Those who cheer for "The O'Reilly Factor" on the Fox News Channel apparently are among a significant number of Americans who prefer a radio-talk-show style of TV commentary. That's their call. More heat than light seems to be generated.

Cartoons such as Wilkinson's , caricaturing Islamic parochial schools as dens of anti-American subversion, serve as a reminder that free speech guarantees neither taste nor accuracy. As I ruminated about it throughout the day, looking for some nuanced or deeper meaning, I decided that, while Wilkinson's intention may have been to criticize vouchers for religious schools in general, the stereotypes in the cartoon conveyed religious bigotry. Cal Thomas used "selected" proof texts from the Quran to demonstrate that Islam is an imperialistic religion, much as he uses proof texts from the Christian Bible to shore up his own brand of quasi-fundamentalism. Nonsense dominated the morning editorial section.

I am not an expert in Islam, nor one qualified to interpret the Quran, but I do know something about religion in North America 2001 and the experience of immigrant religious groups in U.S. history. I prefer to use Sharon, Mass. as a point of departure for getting a fix on Islam.

In her book, *A New Religious America* (2001), Harvard comparative-religion professor Diana Eck discusses the Sharon scene. I recommend her chapter on Islam for a brief, clear and informative read. There are between 6 and 6.5 million Muslims in the United States. Between 25 percent and 40 percent are African Americans. That means Islam is now our second-largest faith tradition. Islam in America is itself diverse. The New England Center is composed of Muslims born in more than 30 countries. There are approximately 1,400 mosques and more than 200 full-time Islamic schools nationwide. Islam is here to stay.

The question being answered by those shaping Islam in the United States is "What does it mean to be both a Muslim and an American?" Other religious groups have had to deal with variations on the same question. The tensions and confusions between ethnicity and religion, between traditional lifestyles and the dominant culture, between commitment and openness will get worked out. One hopes that in the next two generations an authentic version of Islam emerging from its American experience will demonstrate to the world that Islam can flourish in the context of religious freedom and pluralism, even of consumer capitalism.

One might even dare hope that the Sharon example proves to be the model for "an America where Jews and Muslims live together in a free society." In the meantime, we need to reiterate ad nauseam that this terrorism is not Islam. We should remind our Muslim neighbors that others in the past have borne a fear and pain inflicted by those reacting to the Roman catholic "Plot" or the Jewish "Conspiracy." I suspect that what Muslims are bearing will be more severe, but it is not unprecedented. The silver lining is our short attention span when it comes to bigotry. Our scapegoats are also pluralist in character.

—October 6, 2001

PLURALIST AMERICA

Pluralist America

As I have noted a central theme in the columns has been the essentially pluralist character of American religion and culture. It is, therefore, a bit beside the point to designate a chapter as one on pluralist America. The rationale for doing so is that these two columns really center on this theme.

"A whole lot of switching is going on" was occasioned by then Secretary of State Madeleine Albright's late-life discovery that she is Jewish by birth. My takeoff on this interesting story was that Albright's experience was not all that unique in the United States in 1997. We lead the world in "switching" religions.

The second selection, "Religious studies in public universities: 30 years and counting," was written on the occasion of Florida State University Religion Department's 30th -anniversary observance. I was the department chair when I wrote it, and the palpable conflict of interest is admitted up front. A secular department of religious studies in a state university makes obvious sense in a society in which the pluralist character of religion is recognized and by the subsequent affirmation of pluralism as the appropriate public philosophy.

A whole lot of switching is going on

Secretary of State Madeleine Albright didn't score diplomatically with me this past week. In expressing regret for not having time to investigate her Jewish origins, she said, "If I'd been a professor or unemployed, I would have looked into this." In defense of the professoriat, let me insist that we academicians as well are often too busy with important work to deal with painful questions of personal identity.

Fact is, professors, the unemployed, even secretaries of state, all begin with the cards our parents deal us. The hand Madeleine Albright drew identified her as a Roman Catholic of patriotic Czech background. When she married in 1959, she joined the Episcopal Church.

For most of us, the issue is not decisions made in the 1930s by Josef and Mandula Korbel (Albright's parents), but their daughter's public denial of any knowledge of her family history when the story revealing it broke in the *Washington Post* Feb 4. As pundits question and Albright explains, we realize how complicated it all is.

One of the more interesting comments made in the early discussion of this fascinating story was that of Zbigniew Brzezinski, Polish-born national-security adviser in the Carter administration. Brzezinski, assuming that Albright's family members "were probably fairly secular Jews to begin with," noted that Americans "have a very naïve view of the symbiosis and interpenetration between Jewish and non-Jewish populations in Central Europe" prior to World War II.

What was true in Europe between the wars is even more true in the United States in the 1990s. Our nation leads the world in conversions of individuals from one faith tradition or one denomination to another. Sociologists term these conversions "switching."

A lot of switching goes on. Probably more than 30 percent of the people in this country switch denominations or major faith traditions during their lifetime. Many switch more than once. Please note that such switching is just as apt to indicate that the person is serious about religious commitment as to indicate a casualness toward it.

Reasons for passing from one faith tradition to another, to be sure, are different at century's end from what they were in the 1930s or 1940s. Fear of anti-Semitism and concern for the future of one's children have been replaced by an increase in interfaith and interdenominational marriages. There is also less parental influence on religious affiliation and marital decisions than in the past.

For centuries, one more or less inherited the family religion and either took it seriously or let it wane. The principal reality, of course, is the pluralistic character of contemporary society. We have more options than earlier generations had. The grandchildren of a Methodist or Baptist have the option of becoming Muslims, Roman Catholics, Zen Buddhists—or creating their own religion on the Internet.

The interpenetration about which Brzezinski speaks is more intense and widespread than ever. The only way accurately to tell the religious players is with a scorecard in constant revision.

—March 1, 1997

Religious studies in American universities: 30 years and counting

A 30-year anniversary doesn't seem like much of a story, at least not for an academic department in a venerable university. Unlike other disciplines, however, religious studies in public universities have only recently been established. Before the 1960's an institution might have had a "Bible Chair" or a privately financed auxiliary "School of Religion." Other departments might have had a faculty member interested in religion as part of his or her focus on sociology, history, philosophy, or art. But religion was not a coherent, organized field of study.

The introduction of religious studies in public education was occasioned by the Supreme Court's Schempp decision (1963). In Schempp, the Court excluded prayers from public schools, but it also made it clear that there was no constitutional problem with the academic teaching *about* religion. Justice Tom Clark wrote "....it might well be said that one's education is not complete without a study of comparative religion or history of religion...when presented objectively as part of a secular program in education...."

Florida State University, after a preparatory three-year study, established a department of religion in 1965. Thirty years later, it is generally acknowledged to be among the top six or seven departments among public universities in the United States. (I am, of course, a bit short of total objectivity on the subject of our national ranking.) We have 13 faculty positions, enroll 1,000-1,300 students each semester (with approximately 70 undergraduate majors) and have both M.A. and Ph.D. programs offering a concentration in Eastern as well as Western religious traditions.

Thirty years, then, represents the first generation of religious studies in public universities; FSU's religion department is both pioneer and premier in the field. In lower-division, undergraduate courses in liberal studies, we assume that religion should be taught because it plays an important role in human affairs. Religion ought not be the one subject about which an otherwise knowledgeable and literate person is ignorant.

But we go beyond a minimal level of religious literacy to offer our students, particularly our majors, the opportunity to dig deeper into religious thought and behavior, developing their interpretive and critical intelligence.

There is, of course, some risk in subjecting religion to critical inquiry, but there is greater risk in not doing so. In our pluralist society—one characterized by culture wars ("religious wars")—it is urgent that we understand our differences if we are to order our common life and reach working consensus.

Wherever religion has been taught in the United States since World War II, it has experienced substantial enrollments. Some of my friends from both inside and outside of the academy are not surprised that students take religion courses as part of their general education, but they wonder at the number of students who pursue an undergraduate major in religion: "What do you do with a religion major?"

There aren't that many jobs to be found in churches, synagogues, mosques, or teaching in universities. Perhaps half of our undergraduate religion majors are "double majors," an arrangement that accommodates both vocational concerns and intellectual interests. As one of our honors majors—who has a dual major in business and religion—recently put it: "My business major...is a trade degree. Religion is something I'm doing for me."

—February 17, 1994

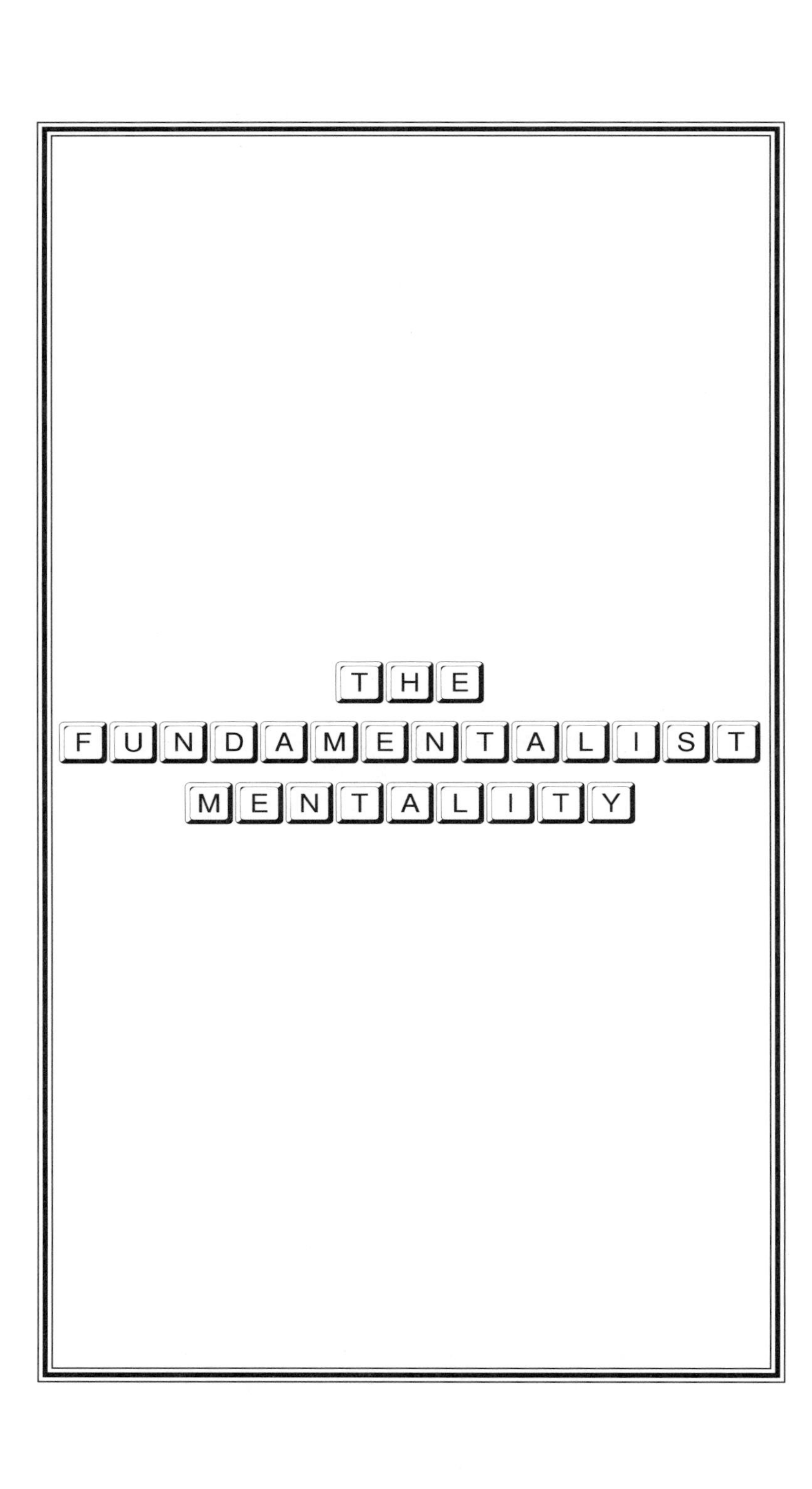
THE
FUNDAMENTALIST
MENTALITY

The Fundamentalist Mentality

I guess a second major theme of *Religion in America* through the years (the first being religious pluralism) is that of questioning religious absolutisms, criticizing them philosophically, theologically, politically, culturally...humanly. Frequently the conversation has involved the concept of "fundamentalism." Two of the columns below use the term. I am aware of problems with the word, but it is hard to shake as a way of getting at a certain type of religious absolutism in American, and now global, religion and culture. I do not use the term pejoratively and, I hope, I use it with decent accuracy and consistency. Although I think religious absolutism is always wrong because no revelation is directly, "nakedly" divine without cultural mediation and that, furthermore, finite creatures are incapable of appropriating absolute truth, I have no quarrel with fundamentalist friends and neighbors except on matters of intolerance.

"What do you mean when you say 'fundamentalist'" was an early column explaining the meaning of fundamentalism as a historical variant within North American Protestantism. I thought it might be helpful to distinguish between other evangelicals and fundamentalists. I remember my irritation when, in 1976, a leading Northeastern intellectual, referred to Jimmy Carter as a fundamentalist. A number of persons, particularly in non-Protestant circles, found the column helpful.

"Absolute certainty is not for everyone" was probably the most confessional column I wrote in sixteen years of *Religion in America.* My epistemological position is that finite human beings do not possess absolute truth. Any "truth" we possess is relative. I laid bare my own religious position as a way of demonstrating that, while one may not believe in absolutes, it is still possible, indeed necessary, to take positions. The issue of absolutes is perhaps the crucial one between fundamentalists and other believers. Faith in God need not entail believing that one's faith is based on absolute knowledge. One can believe in the Absolute without claiming to have absolute knowledge of the object of one's trust.

"The shooting may already have begun," was a column appearing five years later which deals with the "culture wars" theme from the angle that the conviction of absolute certainty can lead to justifying violence. The column was rather widely reprinted, appearing, for instance, on the op-ed page of the Chicago *Tribune* on the following Labor Day.

"The personal and social history of the prince of darkness" was occasioned by a spate of religious literature—both novels and scholarly monographs—dealing with Satan. It coincided with some discussion with twelve-step group members who spoke of their experiences with drug addiction with reference to their sense of the palpable presence of evil: "if there is a higher power, there sure as hell is a lower power." They had experiential arguments for the existence of the devil. One of the reasons for selecting it is to point out that many who use devil talk use it to demonize others.

The inclusion of "Victorian religion and Orlando's magic" deals with the generic opposition of the religious fundamentalist to "modernity." All Southern Baptists are not fundamentalists, but the national convention has been under the tight control of fundamentalists for well over a decade. The Convention's 2000 annual meeting in Orlando was an essayist's dream. The fundamentalist foray into the Magic kingdom proved an occasion to compare and contrast opposing cultural worlds.

As the selection which opens this anthology was the first column in "Religion in America," so "Shall the fundamentalists win?" was among the last of the columns written to date. The operative qualifier is *militant.* There are passive fundamentalists who just want to be, more or less, left alone. It is from the ranks of the militant fundamentalists that terrorists are recruited.

What do you mean when you say "fundamentalist?"

Using evangelical" and "fundamentalist" interchangeably is a common error that blurs important distinctions among Protestant Christians in America. A recent example of such murky writing was a story the *Tallahassee Democrat* printed July 6, written by a member of Knight-Ridder's Washington bureau. The reporter used the term "evangelical" repeatedly when he spoke of fundamentalist groups. His definitions of evangelical Christians were not very helpful.

"So what's the point, Professor?" Well, the point is that not all evangelicals are fundamentalists. Fundamentalism is a distinct version of evangelical Christianity, with its own unique history.

First, a word about evangelicalism. Evangelical Christianity is rooted in a late 17th century movement called pietism, historically associated with the Moravians in Germany and the Methodists in Great Britain. Pietists objected to the conventional, laid-back acceptance of inherited tradition in the established religions of the time. They wanted a religion of conviction based on firsthand experience. They emphasized the emotions—the heart, not the head.

Pietism starts with an emphasis on the Bible's authority and personal religious experience. That personal experience includes the conviction of guilt, the experience of forgiveness, conversion (being "born again"), living a holy life within the fellowship of Christian community. It is, finally, characterized by the free expression of faith in hymns (as contrasted with liturgical worship), testimony and evangelical endeavor, that is sharing the faith with others.

Where the questions for the state churches might be, "Do you subscribe to the Augsburg Confession (or the Westminster Confession)?," the key question for the pietists was, "Do you know Jesus Christ as your personal savior?"

Up to the Civil War, the dominant religion in America was Protestant evangelicalism, an American version of pietism. The large Methodist, Baptist, and Disciples of Christ denominations were shaped by Colonial and frontier expressions of pietistic revivalism. This American evangelicalism also was quite influential among the Presbyterians and in a number of other church bodies. But after the Civil War, immigration, urbanization and popular public education led to a great ferment in American religion. Millions of immigrants were not Anglo-Saxon Protestants, so the evangelical majority was threatened. The United States experienced an unprecedented population shift to urban life, whereas the Protestant experience had been very much a small-town and country affair. Critical historical scholarship undermined traditional notions of church doctrine and biblical authority. After Darwin, evolutionary naturalism threatened to replace the synthesis between supernatural religion and Victorian morality.

Many evangelicals revised their understanding of the faith along more liberal lines and became mainline Protestants. But others were concerned that the "acids of modernity," to use Walter Lippman's phrase, were eroding traditional religious faith. They began what was to be known as the fundamentalist movement.

The term "fundamentalist" probably is derived from a series of booklets titled, *The Fundamentals: A Testimony of Truth*, published in 1910. The twin emphases of the movement were the supernatural origin of Scripture, expressed in the new doctrine of the Bible's inerrancy in all detail, and the supernatural aspects of Christ's person and work. Fundamentalists, then, must affirm the following propositions:

- The inerrancy of Scripture.
- Original sin and universal depravity.
- The virgin birth of Christ.
- The "substitutionary atonement" of Christ for our sins. That means the only true understanding of the crucifixion is that of Christ dying as our substitute to make satisfaction for our sins.
- The physical resurrection of Christ.
- The physical return of Christ, to set up a millennial kingdom on earth.

While most evangelicals subscribe to some or all of the above, the point is that fundamentalists emphasize doctrinal purity rather than the more subjective experience of the warm heart. In their focus on correct doctrine, fundamentalists betray the essential pietistic emphasis.

After World War I, the fundamentalists increased their efforts to turn America back to God. They waged a holy war and experienced a decisive defeat. The symbolic final battle occurred in the Dayton, Tenn., "monkey trial" in 1925. There William Jennings Bryan's last stand against teaching biological evolution in public schools signaled the fundamentalists' failure to capture the leadership of mainline denominations and to convert a godless society to supernatural truth.

In disarray they withdrew from high visibility and regrouped. They worked largely through independent denominations, congregations, Bible institutes and other autonomous organizations. Their center of gravity shifted from the North to the South, where the religious and cultural climate was more congenial to fundamentalist activities. They tended to be separatist and politically dormant.

Since the late 1970s, fundamentalists have become increasingly militant and politically mobilized. The enemy is modernism or "secular humanism," a code term for a human-centered world view that has no room for God.

In Hawkins County, Tenn., the parents suing the school board over books used in the schools are fundamentalists; many of their neighbors who feel they have gone too far are evangelicals. All Southern Baptists are evangelicals; the militants who have seized control of Southern Baptist Convention committees are fundamentalists. Both Jimmy Carter and Jerry Falwell are evangelicals; of the two, only Falwell is a fundamentalist. There really is a dime's worth of difference.

—August 2, 1986

Absolute certainty is not for everyone

I marvel at people who are absolutely certain they are correct on the issue of abortion or the death penalty. The key word is "absolutely." Such certainty is too high for me to attain. I cannot think of one of my opinions or any of my "truths" that I believe to be infallible. My tentativeness does not prevent me from serious commitments, but you won't see me with a bumper sticker asserting, "God said it; I believe it; that settles it."

I am, for instance, one of the small minority of Floridians who oppose the death penalty. The ultimate basis for my opposition is theological. I am, however, willing to grant that a cogent and morally respectable argument exists in support of capital punishment in extreme cases. Such a stance has meant that I displease not only those who disagree with me on the issue, but sometimes also those who agree, but distrust my lack of absolutism.

Since I'm in a confessing mood, I'll go ahead and risk losing half of my readership by saying I am pro-choice regarding abortion. I am not all that comfortable with my position. I envy some of my pro-life friends for their settled position, and I'm much closer to their view than that of many pro-choice folk. I have been booed by militant feminists and written off by those who accuse me of wanting to send every woman who has an abortion on a guilt trip—because I have argued that abortions are, at best, tragic events that are always to be viewed as morally serious decisions.

There are advantages to being identified with infallible opinions. Psychological certainty usually is a corollary of intellectual and moral certainty. So one can feel settled and secure in a world of moral absolutes. I suspect it is also less work to operate from a base of absolute truth. It is wearying always to be revisiting issues and revising our positions. And it does take energy to really listen to other opinions.

But there are advantages, both personal and societal, to having a bit of humility about one's convictions. For starters, it elevates the quality of conversation. One cannot so easily stereotype the opponent or oversimplify his position. Sloganeering ceases to serve as a substitute for serious moral discourse.

It is inaccurate, on the one hand, to label as "pro-abortion" someone who believes that the intentional termination of a pregnancy can be a morally responsible decision. Such labeling is similar to asserting that someone is pro-divorce, or pro-nephrectomy or pro-hurricane. Such a person is pro-choice, not pro-abortion. It is simplistic, on the other hand, to assert that "control over one's body" is a moral absolute that should end all further discussion. If there is a difference between a fetus and, say, a wart or an appendix, then more analysis is needed.

Another advantage to a decent humility concerning one's viewpoint is that it permits one to modify or change an opinion. Infallibility is a bit inconvenient if you decide you were wrong. Allowing that any genuine issue has at least two sides (that's what makes it an issue) tends to free us from the scourge of contemporary American public life: single-issue politics.

The litmus-test approach to politics may be effective in the short run, but it does little for the ongoing quality of policy formation. There is a linkage between absolutism and fanaticism. It is the human tendency to identify an important cause as the all-important cause.

Some of you are saying, "Sandon, you think all truth is relative anyway." Well, yeah, in a way. I believe all human thought is limited and unfinished. Being a "creature," a word that logically implies belief in a creator, means our status is finite. That includes human thinking.

I cannot possess absolute truth. Truth in everyday life, therefore, is provisional, never total. I can live with probabilities well enough without having to know everything. This is not to say I do not believe in an absolute. As a matter of faith I believe in *the* absolute, the One beyond the many, as the philosophers say. But my knowledge of the Absolute One is far from absolute. God alone is omniscient.

To use old-timey theological language, I believe in the sovereignty of God alone. Everything else is relative, and to elevate another value to the level of God is idolatry. For many of us, therefore, the real truth vouchsafed to the teaching magistracy of the church—the papal office in Catholicism, for instance—is not infallible.

Sacred scripture, though central to the life of a community of faith, is not inerrant in all matters. Theological doctrines and moral norms, as useful as they often are and as seriously as I take them, are not absolutes.

This preachy essay is no brief for continually suspended judgment. We must all take positions and serve causes if we are to be morally responsible persons. But each of us views reality from a particular standpoint. Only God's perspective is universal. All divine truth is appropriated by human comprehension, held in what St. Paul termed earthen vessels—clay pots.

Maybe we serve God and neighbor best when we lower our voices and listen to those who don't share our certainties. Perhaps conviction is more religious when it is accompanied by openness and a touch of humility. I am absolutely certain it is. Perhaps.

—February 11, 1989

The shooting may already have begun

"Culture wars always precede shooting wars," University of Virginia sociologist James Davison Hunter reminds us in his new book, *Before the Shooting Begins.* The obvious question is, "Has the shooting *already* begun?" Hunter's latest book is a follow-up to his 1991 book, *Culture Wars: The Struggle to Define America.* Hunter has been arguing that cultural conflict in the United States is "rooted in different systems of moral understanding."

Pat Buchanan, in his speech to the 1992 Republican National Convention, identified theses conflicts as ultimately "a religious war going on for the soul of America." Buchanan is correct if one defines religion by the way it functions in human life. Religion is the way a group deals with the ultimate questions of human existence. Religion, so defined, is the heart of culture, and thus these culture wars are, finally, religious wars over seemingly incompatible first principles. When we start from unreconcilable first principles it is very difficult, if not impossible, to agree on how we are to order our common life.

Hunter uses abortion as a case study to demonstrate the character of our conflicts. The controversy over abortion, he argues, finally "signifies different propositions about what it means to be human." Hunter notes that such incompatible convictions vying with each other to prevail in public policy can lead from tension to conflict to violence. He is of the opinion that "America is still some way off from large-scale civil strife and open violence." I am not so sure.

The shooting of abortion providers in Pensacola, as well as in Wichita, Kan. are indeed violent acts. So are the vandalizing and burning of abortion clinics. Pro-life activists of course, point to violence visited on millions of unborn children. Gustav Niebuhr, religious writer for *The New York Times*, in a recent article pondered "how religions that teach peace can be taken by some adherents to justify acts of violence and bloodshed."

Religions have been in the business of legitimating violence for some time now. Paul Hill, indicted for the recent Pensacola murders, is confident that killing abortion providers is theologically justified. If you are certain that you know and are doing God's will, the end justifies the means. You can employ traditional Just War theory to justify killing abortion providers if you start with the premise that abortion is murder. When one moves from belief to fanaticism, nuance and ambiguity receive short shrift. Reality becomes black and white, the other person becomes either all good or all bad (please note, I am speaking of pro-life extremists , not all pro-life activists).

Where do we go from here? We have to step back if we are going to go forward. I suggest that we not look to national political or religious leaders for direction. The testimony of two Missouri women, cited by Hunter, one a pro-life activist and one an abortion-clinic director, offer more hope for a useable future. Says the activist, "No one is ever going to convince me that it is all right to kill unborn babies, and I'm going to go on working to make abortion illegal. But that doesn't mean we need to demonize each other...we have to sit down and talk with each other. " Says the clinic director, "It has become very clear to me that the polarization I have engaged in for years has not served the women in my community, has not helped to resolve anything and was a self-indulgence."

From such stuff common ground is identified and then occupied. Civility and substantive argument are reclaimed. There is no way around these wars but there is a way through them: quiet and thoughtful conversation.

—August 20, 1994

The personal and social history of the Prince of Darkness

Much of my summer agenda has included the reading list from hell, so to speak. The subjects of evil and the devil seem to have replaced those of saints and angels on the best-selling lists.

I have read Elaine Pagels' *The Origin of Satan* and Robert Fuller's *Naming the Antichrist: The History of An American Obsession.* I am just finishing Anne Rice's latest novel, *Memnoch the Devil.* All three books were published this year by secular trade houses.

Pagels, a religion professor at Princeton, reviews the idea of Satan from its obscure origins in the Hebrew Bible to its Christian New Testament meaning of evil incarnate, the cosmic enemy of God and humanity. She demonstrates that, because Christians read the gospels and identified with the first-century disciples, "for some two thousand years they have also identified their opponents, whether Jews, pagans or heretics, with forces of evil, and so with Satan."

The idea of the Antichrist, mentioned only four times in the New Testament, came to mean "the ultimate enemy of Christ who will appear in the final chapter of history to lead the forces of Satan in one last desperate battle against the forces of God." Robert Fuller, a religion professor at Bradley University, traces the social history of the idea of the Antichrist in America from the Colonial Puritans to Hal Lindsey's "The Late Great Planet Earth."

Cotton Mather, the eminent 17th-century Puritan divine and intellectual, was convinced that Satan had beaten the Puritans to the New World and had long since claimed dominion over the native Americans, Satan's miserable minions. Other candidates for the Antichrist in the American experience have included the pope, Freemansonry, deists, FDR and, most recently, computer technology, as in *Fiber Optics: The Eye of the Antichrist.*

Anne Rice, in her surrealistic novel, seeks to drive the reader to deal with the problem of belief in, and subsequent service to, either God or the devil. Her novel reminds us that many persons experience an encounter with evil that seems to be more than subjective projection.

I recall a conversation with a member of Narcotics Anonymous who was struggling with the Twelve Step Movement's second step: the testimony of members that they have come "to believe that a power greater than ourselves (can) restore us to sanity." The N.A. member told me,

"I can tell you that, if there is a higher power, there is also a lower power. It is just as real and it is terrifying." Such persons experience evil not just as the absence of the good. It is in an adversarial relationship with the good.

Why the current interest in Satan? Perhaps people are a bit tired of "being embraced by the light" and working on positive mental attitudes and are looking for a little balance. More seriously, the problem of evil is fundamental and enduring. The human condition, one might argue, has not changed that much since John Milton wrote *Paradise Lost*. Even more seriously, there seems to be an increased tendency for various divisions of our current culture wars to demonize the opposition.

Is the demonic a "He" or an "It?" "He" (or "She") may say too much; "It" may say too little. One thing for certain: We should avoid "they."

—August 12, 1995

Victorian religion and Orlando's magic

It's not so much what they said but where they said it. A denomination whose official positions construct a bastion of Victorian Protestant Fundamentalism was meeting in Orlando—arguably the global center of popular culture. What a dramatic setting for a culture-war confrontation.

In one sense, the story of this past week's annual meeting of the Southern Baptist Convention was something of a yawner. To be sure, denomination leaders guided the delegates (known as messengers) into a revision of the Baptist Faith and Message Statement. Specifically, the statement opposes homosexuality, pornography, adultery, abortion, and "all manner of deviant and pagan sexuality." As expected, the addition to the document that the office of pastor is to be limited to men passed without debate. All of this is perfectly consistent with the direction the Convention has been taking for more than two decades.

But ironies abound in the Southern Baptist movement toward doctrinal conformity. What precisely is the authority of such a document in a tradition that is proudly non-creedal and with authority vested in the absolute autonomy of each congregation? Presumably the approximately 100 women who now serve as pastors or co-pastors in Southern Baptist congregations will continue to do so. What, finally, is the meaning of orthodoxy in a denomination that has always strongly emphasized the doctrine of soul competency—the conviction that every "soul" should deal directly and personally with God, with each individual ultimately his or her own interpreter?

One clue to the cultural component of the Convention's agenda is found in a statement by the Rev. Adrian Rogers, former Convention president and chair of the committee that drafted the revision. "Many denominations are being swept up by the culture," he stated—but not, he argued, the Southern Baptists. A revealing and underreported Convention resolution was one against "the threat of New Age globalism." Such globalism, according to the resolution, is based on the philosophy of secular humanism and "poses a threat to the traditional family." Read *Victorian family.*

Comparing the experiences of Disney and the Southern Baptist Convention is instructive. Uncle Walt's original vision was also one of nostalgia for Victorian-American culture. But Disney Inc. was evolving, even before Michael Eisner's appointment as CEO in 1984, into a global media empire that championed more of a pragmatic than an absolute value system. Those of us who've been in Florida the past three decades have seen Orlando's transformation from a town-and-country citrus culture to a global center for transportation, communications and marketing opportunities.

The Southern Baptist leadership hasn't moved from its Victorian vision. In its "New Age Globalism" resolution, it warns, "Scripture teaches that God has marked the times and boundaries of the nations of the earth." For fundamentalists, geopolitical arrangements, social roles, history and texts are frozen. This position is the basis for the Southern Baptists' quarrel with Disney and the motive for their quixotic attempt to boycott Disney three years ago.

Southern Baptists made a foray into enemy territory and took their stand. One hopes there are options other than nineteenth-century fundamentalism and Magic Kingdom fantasies.

—June 17, 2000

Shall the fundamentalists win?

The question in the headline is the title of a famous sermon preached by the Rev. Harry Emerson Fosdick in 1922. Its context was the fundamentalist controversy that divided North American Protestantism in the twentieth century. Fosdick was concerned that the fundamentalist program was "essentially illiberal and intolerant." He was determined that evangelicals who where not fundamentalists, particularly those who were Baptists and Presbyterians, not be driven from mainline churches.

The context has changed, but Fosdick's question is perhaps more urgent today than it was in the 1920s. It needs refining: "Shall the militant fundamentalists win?" It is from the ranks of militant religious fundamentalists that terrorists are recruited. Certainly not all militant fundamentalists are terrorists, but all who are terrorists in the name of God (or a sectarian tradition) come from various religious fundamentalisms. All major faith traditions and their primary subsets have fundamentalist variants: Christian, Muslim, Jewish, Hindu, Sikh and Theravada Buddhist as well as others.

I am aware of problems with the term "fundamentalist." But I use it because no other word is as serviceable for cross-cultural, journalistic and popular educational communication. A newspaper column allows for neither the discussion of more precise alternative concepts nor for the extensive review of possible misuses.

Fundamentalists rally around selected fundamental truths of their religion that they believe are absolute and unchanging. Those fundamentalists who belong to religions "of the book"—notably Jews, Protestant Christians and Muslims—usually believe in the inerrancy of their sacred texts. Another distinctive feature of fundamentalists is their rejection of modernity, particularly of secular Western culture, the "modernism" of choice these days.

Historians Martin E. Marty and R. Scott Appleby, editors of the five-volume *Fundamentalist Project*, observe that fundamentalists are fighters. They fight back against that which challenges their core identity. They fight for an absolute worldview that they believe they have inherited—one, at any rate, that they certainly have adopted. They fight with their own interpretations of concepts taken from their tradition: Global Jihad, for instance. While opposing the modern scientific worldview, they are not averse to using modern technology to wage their fight. They fight against others, the enemies of the true faith, at times including co-religionists whom they identify as compromisers, or, God forbid, moderates. They fight under God, finally, convinced that they are commissioned to carry out God or Allah's will against "them."

Fundamentalist preacher Jerry Falwell, interestingly enough, apologized for the timing, but not the content, of post-9/11 remarks in which he blamed an assortment of liberals for being partially responsible for the disasters. Falwell specified gays and lesbians, the ACLU, abortionists and those who have removed God from the public square as the enemies: "All of them who have tried to secularize America—I point the finger in the face and say, 'You helped this to happen.'"

Falwell, of course, is not a terrorist, but pointing the finger in the face and pointing the gun at the enemy evidence a common hostile premise. Before the shooting begins, there has to be the cultivation of a mindset and the compiling of enemies lists.

For the militant fundamentalists to win, all that is necessary is for their co-religionists to be indifferent to their activities. It is not enough for the Islamic world to denounce officially the attacks. It must also engage fundamentalist leadership in the interpretation of Islam. American Muslims must be attentive to militant fundamentalist influence in some of their communities. Islamic regimes must stop looking the other way and engage fundamentalist movements before they themselves are toppled by terrorist revolution. The White House shouldn't just rebuke Falwell; the Republican Party should refuse to be bullied by a religious right that doesn't speak for that many Americans in the first place.

The struggle is not so much between faith traditions or civilizations. It is between those believers who proclaim that their version is the one that is absolutely correct to the exclusion of all others and those who believe that no religious party holds the patent on correct interpretation.

—November 3, 2001

Index